SKULL SESSION

SKULL SESSION

MASTERING THE MENTAL GAME IN SPORTS, WORK, AND LIFE

SCOTT COCHRAN
with **IVAN MAISEL**

NEW YORK   NASHVILLE

Copyright © 2025 by Scott Cochran
Cover design by Jay Smith, Juicebox Designs
Cover copyright © 2025 by Hachette Book Group, Inc.

Hachette Book Group supports the right to free expression and the value of copyright. The purpose of copyright is to encourage writers and artists to produce the creative works that enrich our culture.

The scanning, uploading, and distribution of this book without permission is a theft of the author's intellectual property. If you would like permission to use material from the book (other than for review purposes), please contact Permissions@hbgusa.com. Thank you for your support of the author's rights.

Center Street
Hachette Book Group
1290 Avenue of the Americas
New York, NY 10104
centerstreet.com
@CenterStreet

First Edition: August 2025

Center Street is a division of Hachette Book Group, Inc. The Center Street name and logo are registered trademarks of Hachette Book Group, Inc.

The publisher is not responsible for websites (or their content) that are not owned by the publisher.

Center Street books may be purchased in bulk for business, educational, or promotional use. For information, please contact your local bookseller or email the Hachette Book Group Special Markets Department at Special.Markets@hbgusa.com.

Library of Congress Cataloging-in-Publication Data has been applied for.

ISBN: 978-1-546-00973-3 (hardcover); 978-0-316-59732-6 (ebook)

Printed in the United States of America

LSC-H

Printing 1, 2025

*To my wife, Cissy, and our children,
Beau, Savannah, and Lucy.*

*Your love and support motivate me
to stay strong in my sobriety.*

*And to all the players I've coached.
I learned more from you than I ever
could have taught you.*

CONTENTS

1. Skull Session 1
2. Your Organization's DNA 15
3. Beginnings 37
4. Coach Saban 51
5. SMART Goals 67
6. Be Where Your Feet Are 77
7. Addiction 89
8. The Road to Recovery 111
9. Love, Not Fear 133
10. Positive Self-Talk 151
11. Catfishing Your Way to Leadership 161
12. Head Coach 175
    Acknowledgments 181
    About the Authors 183

ONE

SKULL SESSION

When I left the University of Alabama in January 2020 after thirteen seasons as head strength coach, conditioning coach, and motivational master for Crimson Tide football, I had six national championship rings, enough celebrity to be doing regional TV ads, and an alter ego: Coach Yeah! I went through conditioning work yelling *"Yeah! Yeah! Yeah! Yeah! Yeah!"* at epic decibel levels, cheering on my players, cheering up my players, getting them psyched enough to perform at skill levels they didn't know they could reach.

I also had a huge chemical dependency. I was hooked on oxycodone, *oxy* for short, and Adderall.

SKULL SESSION

I had been hooked for almost eight years. I had hidden my addiction from everyone: head coach Nick Saban; trainer Jeff Allen, who was and is like a brother to me; the other coaches on the staff. I had hidden it from my wife, Cissy, whom I fell in love with pretty much the moment she walked into my weight room. I hid it from my friend Steve Sarkisian, now the head coach at Texas, when he worked at Alabama in 2016 and in 2019. Steve is in recovery himself, and he never suspected a thing.

I left Alabama to work for my close friend Kirby Smart, the head coach at Georgia. Kirby worked for Coach Saban for eleven years. Kirby and I were tight; our wives were tight; our children were close. Kirby didn't know about my addiction, either.

Three months after I changed jobs, it was just another Friday morning in Tuscaloosa. Well, not just another. For one thing, it was April 10, 2020—Good Friday, for those of you looking for greater meaning. For another, we were a month into the COVID-19 pandemic lockdowns, which is why I had returned to Tuscaloosa from my new job in Athens. Once the coaches couldn't go into the office, it made more sense for me and Cissy and our three kids to hunker down in the house we hadn't sold yet.

And, oh yeah, one more thing: That's the morning that my addiction tried to kill me and damn near did.

I left Alabama to go work for Kirby because I wanted to get out of the weight room. I wanted to be a coach on the field. At least, that's the story that got out in the public, and I didn't try to correct it. The real reason I left Alabama is that I thought a change of venue would help me stop taking oxy. I had all these people around me getting me the pills I needed. Maybe if I left, I wouldn't have access, and I could stop. That's called running from your addiction, and it's about as effective as it sounds. My addiction ran right alongside me. It turned out there are people in Georgia who have pills, too.

Like a lot of people suddenly working from home, I proclaimed the kids' upstairs playroom as my workspace. We had a computer in there, so I could have Zoom meetings with my Georgia coaching staff in there without being disrupted by whatever was going on in the house. I moved a big living room chair in there to make it feel more like an office, the girls' dolls notwithstanding. On this particular morning, our girls, Savannah and Lucy, were outside, and our son, Beau, was in the basement.

SKULL SESSION

Toward the end of my time at Alabama, someone gave me an Opana, which is oxycodone mixed with morphine. When my body discovered Opana, my body no longer needed all those oxy pills. I was awesome all day long, until I wasn't. Then I wanted more Opana, too. I got a prescription for Opana. I filled it on the sixteenth of the month. Here it was, April 10, six days short of when I should have been out of pills, and I was out of pills.

I called one of the guys that I always got pills from—that sounds so much more innocent than "my dealer"—and he said, "I can't get you anything. The only thing I can get you is from a guy that I don't trust."

Like an addict is going to hear that.

"I don't give a damn," I said. "I'm sick. I need something. You've got to get this for me. I will pay double."

My guy tried again.

"I'm telling you, dude, I don't trust this guy," he said. "It's got to be something bad."

My addiction wouldn't take no for an answer. I went to the ATM, got some cash, met my guy, and got the pills, which were counterfeit oxycodone with a side order of fentanyl, a drug even more dangerous than oxy. The next morning, Good Friday, I had a Zoom meeting with the Atlanta Falcons' special teams staff.

I prepared a speedball. I chopped up three 30-milligram pills of oxy, mixed in one Adderall, and snorted the four together. I remember the meeting. I killed it. We had a good meeting.

And then Cissy brought me back from the dead.

You could see into the playroom from the stairs, and how lucky that I had not closed the playroom door. Cissy happened to walk upstairs with a basket of laundry, looked in, and saw me slumped over in my big chair. She raced in and tried to straighten me up. I was sweating profusely and turning blue. She started yelling for Beau to help her, and she and I both thank God he didn't hear her. No thirteen-year-old should see a parent overdosing.

Cissy called 911, and as she talked to the operator, she lifted my head and kept trying to pull me back against the chair. I regained consciousness, sort of. Cissy described it as if I were coming out of surgery. I was conscious but in La-La Land, not making any sense, and my breathing was labored. I stood, still sweating up a storm, and made it to the shower. Cissy ended the 911 call and called James

Robinson, the Alabama team doctor. He couldn't make sense out of it. "He's blue, like he isn't breathing?" he asked.

Dr. Robinson wasn't in his office that day, but Brett Bentley was. Cissy got me dressed and drove me over to the student center. I got in there, and they could barely find a pulse, so they hooked me up to oxygen. Dr. Bentley showed Cissy some Narcan and said, "I think he's taken something. I don't know what it is."

Cissy called a neighbor and asked her to go upstairs to see if she could find any pill bottles. She went in there and found the pills and flushed them down the toilet. Dr. Bentley began to talk to Cissy about rehab facilities.

"I don't recommend you keeping him home over the weekend," Dr. Bentley told her. And then, almost as an aside, he said, "This is not going to be easy."

Dr. Bentley was right about that. It was hell. I mean, absolute hell.

You don't become the dominant program in the nation without drawing on resilience. Our teams at Alabama proved that they knew how to come back, never more so than in the national championship game at the end of the 2017 season. That's the one where Georgia mauled us in the first half, jumping to a 13–0 lead. Coach Saban benched quarterback Jalen Hurts in the second half and put freshman Tua Tagovailoa on the field. Tua brought us back from two touchdowns behind and won in overtime with that iconic 41-yard touchdown pass to classmate DeVonta Smith.

I know something about comebacks. I have been to a rehab facility three times, one visit a hundred-day stay that really changed my life. Over and above the physical difficulty of withdrawal, I had to deal with being away from my family for such a long time. From the time our children were born, I had never been in a situation where I couldn't go home to them. I had that voice in my head, asking if I could really stay sober. I leaned on my experience of leading young people toward a goal. Under Coach Saban and under Kirby, we coached our players to perform their job, not to worry about the result. We taught them not to look at the scoreboard. Look at your opponent lined up in front of you. That is your task. That mindset is exactly what you have to learn in rehab. You can't worry about never taking another pill for the rest of your life. You have to focus on not taking a pill today.

Every day is a fight, a choice. I choose to win. What I've learned is that success isn't about championships or money or accolades, all three of which I have chased. Success is about integrity. It's about the person you are when no one is watching. It's lifting that last rep, running that last set of stadium stairs. Every morning, I look in the mirror and ask myself, "Am I proud of me?" Most days, I am. But I have to earn that pride again in the day unfolding before me. And again the day after that.

Because I had trained players to think that way, I always have the belief, the faith, that my recovery is going to succeed. I just need to keep grinding. This is going to work. I'll be able to stay sober. I'll be able to live a life in recovery. Some of that is "fake it until you make it," although I prefer to say "fake it until you *become* it." That sounds more rooted, more permanent.

That thinking is an example of a Skull Session. It's a name I picked up from Gayle Hatch, the former Olympic weightlifting coach and a Louisiana legend. After workouts, we'd gather and reflect not just on the physical work, but on the mental and emotional training, too—the why behind the work. When I got to Alabama, I made the name Skull Session my own. Coach Saban called it "mental development and education," but to the players, that sounded like eating kale. So I called it a Skull Session. I brought the same training to Georgia. Champions aren't built in the gym alone. They're built between the ears. They're built by asking yourself hard questions, deciding who you want to be.

We won two more national championships in my time at Georgia. I left the Dawgs' staff after the 2023 season, left big-time college football, content with the idea that I might not coach again. Let me put a finer point on that: might not coach *football* again. Coaching is what I do.

Helping people recover is coaching. I joined with Jeff Breedlove, a former Georgia state legislator who is also in recovery, to form the American Addiction Recovery Association. Our slogan is "Eliminate the Whisper." We want to shatter the stigma attached to addiction and help America understand that addiction is a disease.

Helping business leaders find methods to pull their teams in the right direction is coaching.

Teaching you the methods we used at Alabama and Georgia to attain our goals is coaching.

In *Skull Session*, I'll explain how an average high school athlete became an integral part of eight national champions, how I filled my motivational toolbox with the right gear to turn athletically gifted boys into high-achieving men, and how I beat back the disease of addiction and began coaching football again. After a year away from the game, I am the head coach at the University of West Alabama, a Division II school. I have hired a bunch of my former Alabama players to coach on my staff. They know how I think. They know how champions work.

I know it's a miracle that I'm alive. But when I describe it, it really smacks me upside the head. There are so many ways that I am lucky.

I am an addict who up until today has survived my addiction. I say that because I don't take tomorrow for granted.

I am an addict who has survived my addiction without harming anyone else, either my loved ones or a stranger who had the misfortune to drive near me when I was racing to get high. Thank God I never hurt anybody. That's why my relationship with God is so close, because I easily could have been that guy. I remember driving to a leadership retreat at Sweet Apple Farms after I had ingested too many pills. It's a forty-five-minute drive from the Tuscaloosa campus, and I was freaked out because I was about to nod off and I had a colleague in the car. I pulled over and said, "Dude, why don't you drive? I need to get on the phone." That day scarred me.

I am an addict who would be high on fentanyl and have to drive my kids somewhere. I would start doing the math in my head—*I won't be back before I start to get withdrawal symptoms, so I need to take extra before I get in the car so that I don't get sick.* That's how crazy it is. That's how crazy I was.

I am an addict who has been able to return to my chosen profession, who has learned to delineate between what's important about my work and what isn't. I love the fact that I have been a part of eight national championship teams. I love the fact that I worked at the very top of my sport. But I am completely happy coaching Division II football because what's important to me is the connection I make with young athletes who want to compete and make themselves better.

SKULL SESSION

I am an addict who emerged to do what I feel like God put me on earth to do.

Why did I survive? I like to think that God spared me for a purpose, which is a powerful incentive for me to remain clean. This book is called *Skull Session* because this training has helped me win my biggest game. The book reflects the essential components of a Skull Session—principles such as gratitude, purpose, resilience, and self-discipline. It's about bringing the same energy to your mental work that you do to the weight room. It's about facing yourself, building from the inside out. It's about building a team, a division, an entire corporation, with the traits that will lead you to achieve your goals. It's about doing the work every day, even when you're losing, even when you're in a rehab facility fighting to reclaim your life.

Honestly, I know how lucky I am. I feel as if I have been put here to coach. Everything I've learned—from coaching All-Americans, from my own failures, from my road back to coaching—is in this book. I've got eight rings, I've coached three Heisman Trophy winners and too many first-round draft picks to count, but my proudest moment didn't happen on the field. It's being here, telling my story, helping people make today count. *Skull Session* has a whole lot of football, but my subject is making the best of what life hands you. I'm living proof that life is not about falling. It's about getting up.

TWO

YOUR ORGANIZATION'S DNA

Here's a universal truth about organizations: No matter what the purpose, be it a football team, a fast-food restaurant, or a widget maker, the people in the organization have to know and buy into that purpose. They can't do that until you define the organization's core beliefs and its mission statement.

Core beliefs are your organization's DNA traits. You have to establish your beliefs in order to define the culture in your building. Your DNA traits make you who you are. You've got to have them every day, especially in today's college football, when there's less trickle-down from one season to the next. Your DNA traits instill your players with the character and integrity to represent the program.

At Alabama, our core beliefs under Coach Saban included, in alphabetical order, commitment, discipline, effort, pride, and toughness. At Georgia, Kirby established the core beliefs of composure, connection, resilience, and toughness.

It's football. Toughness is universal.

A perfect example of a core belief is what Chick-fil-A did almost twenty-five years ago. They went to the Ritz-Carlton hotels to learn how their people pamper their guests. Ritz-Carlton is all about hospitality, and Chick-fil-A wanted to adopt those methods and apply them to a fried chicken breast topped by two slices of pickle. What Chick-fil-A took away, with Ritz-Carlton's blessing, is a two-word statement: "My pleasure." When a customer asks for something, or says thank you, at Chick-fil-A, like at a Ritz-Carlton, the response is, "My pleasure." The statement is simple, clear, and definitive. Chick-fil-A created a culture of hospitality with just two words. The service is still fast, but now there's a standard. Your culture is set, and your standard is set by your words: These are our DNA traits.

YOUR ORGANIZATION'S DNA

Every spring, we teach our core beliefs to our players. We'll schedule a week of Skull Sessions on one word, one trait. We'll define it in quick and easily digestible language. For instance, having discipline means doing what you're supposed to do, when you're supposed to do it, the way it's supposed to be done. Commitment is not just pledging to give everything you have to your brothers in the locker room. We explain how it translates to the day-to-day and what that will mean after football. All of our guys understand that they must commit to being on time to workouts and meetings. They understand that because they get physical punishment if they're late. In the real world, you don't have to run sprints if you're late to a meeting. We explain the consequences of a lack of commitment in business. You don't get your work done. You don't make the sale. You get a reputation for being undependable. You don't succeed.

Commitment is simply letting everyone know "I'm all in." You are committed to the process of doing what is necessary to succeed. If you played football on the teams I coached, you're used to winning. You have to show commitment to keep winning.

SKULL SESSION

In that sense, commitment works hand in glove with discipline—the discipline to show up on time; the discipline to do what you're supposed to do; the discipline to put that down, whether *that* is a slice of cake, a phone, a video game, or weed. People use the word *sacrifice* for that kind of decision. You sacrifice to get better. You give something up to get better. That makes it sound harder than it needs to be. What if you change the vocabulary to *invest*? You invest to get better. That makes it positive. You're not giving something up. You're investing. *This is my investment.*

To make the point, we would show the players a video of someone like the late Kobe Bryant, explaining how discipline enabled him to reach the heights he reached in the NBA. To keep them alert and involved, we would ask them questions, like "When did a lack of discipline prevent you from reaching your goals?" And "When did you use discipline to achieve your goals?"

Discipline is not just about abiding by team rules. Discipline is not giving in when all you want to do is stop. We always told our players, "Don't look at the scoreboard. Don't focus on the outcome. Focus on your assignment on this play." When a player gets into his stance, the scoreboard doesn't matter. Along those same lines, we say, "Be a champion," not "We're going to win a championship." Winning is outcome oriented. As much as we would like to think we can control the outcome, we can't. Not 100 percent, anyway. You do everything you're supposed to do, everything you can control, and that's all you can do.

In all my years at Alabama and Georgia, I remember looking at the scoreboard once. In the 2018 national championship game in Santa Clara, my next-to-last season in Tuscaloosa, I knew we were behind Clemson. I looked up and it said 44–16. I had been acting as if the scoreboard doesn't matter. It just makes your life so much easier if you don't focus on "We're behind by this much."

The year before, in our epic overtime victory over Georgia, we were down 13–0 at halftime, and we were getting thrashed. I didn't have to look at the scoreboard. I could see it on our players' faces. I felt as if I needed to say something to everybody.

"I don't want it any other way," I told them. "I don't want the score flipped. I want it just how it is. I want to see if all this work that we've been doing is going to pay off. I believe that it's going to pay off. I just believe, I don't know why. It's crazy, but I just believe if we go out there and play one play at a time, and we stop worrying about the results, I just believe we're going to be fine."

For the rest of the game, I grabbed a towel, and I just kept saying to the players on the sideline, "They're gonna break. They're gonna break. They're gonna break." They did.

It's easy in business to look at the sales goal for the quarter, to think about the year-end bonus, to envision what your new model will mean in your industry once you release it. None of those have anything to do with the task at hand right this minute. If you want to succeed, you have to focus on making that next sale or finding that next bug in the new program. If you do that, the year-end bonus will take care of itself. The new software will change the industry.

Discipline came naturally to me. I was a very disciplined kid in high school. I didn't party. I didn't drink. I didn't do any of that stuff. It was football, football, football. I worked at a video store. My parents owned one for a few years, but I worked at a different one. Other than my hours at the store, everything else in my life revolved around football. Everything, as in I needed to gain weight. Someone told me that in order to gain weight I needed to eat more. When I look back, even for a teenager this is pretty gross. After supper, I would make four sandwiches with Peter Pan creamy peanut butter and strawberry jelly and pour two glasses of chocolate milk. At 10 p.m., I'd eat two of the sandwiches and drink one glass of chocolate milk. Before I went to bed, I'd set my alarm for 2 a.m. When the alarm went off, I would jump up, scarf down the other two PB&Js, drink the other chocolate milk, and go back to sleep. Four hours later, I'd wake up and get ready for my 7 a.m. workout. I started this regimen as a high school sophomore. I kept it up until August of my senior year, and in those two years I went from 190 pounds to 220 pounds. That's sacrifice. That's investment. That's discipline.

My embrace of discipline is one reason I bonded with Coach Saban. My high school coach, J.T. Curtis at John Curtis Christian School in River Ridge, Lousiana, has won more high school football games than anyone ever: 623 victories through the 2024 season. Coach Curtis demanded the same discipline from his players as Coach Saban did. Some people call it tough love. I like that because there is love behind it. Both of them really care about their players, although Coach Saban responded to my love for our players by calling me Father Flanagan. If you're a fan of old movies, you've probably seen Spencer Tracy and Mickey Rooney in the 1938 film *Boys Town*. Tracy played Father Flanagan, who ran the Boys Town orphanage in Nebraska.

I learned from Coach Saban that kids mess up. They make mistakes. When they do, you discipline them. You don't get rid of them. I thought I knew what he really wanted when one of our players failed a drug test or kept missing class. Most assistants would base their reaction on one criterion: Can the guy even help us on the field? No? Get rid of him. Yes? They're like, "He sucks, but we need him."

Coach Saban would always look at me and say, "Father Flanagan? What do you think?"

Maybe it was just me, but I always thought Coach wanted to save these guys. He had saved so many in his first two seasons at Alabama that we should have run off. He could have just wiped them all out. But he didn't want to. He believed that we could develop them. They weren't the best players.

Maybe they could help us on special teams. Maybe they would get a degree.

Even the guys who literally fought me because I made them work so hard, he wanted to try to keep around. After a few seasons, when we had a kid who missed a workout or missed a practice and was battling something, Father Flanagan was going to try to make it all work out. When a kid came through Alabama, Coach Saban believed wholeheartedly that he should leave having become a better person than when he walked in the door. He made sure that would happen through the toughness, through the discipline, through the commitment to excellence, through the effort put in.

Every Monday during the season we had "good, bad and ugly" video from the previous game. We'd show the team the good we did in the game, like how it all came together on this play or that one; the bad, like missed executions, mental errors; and the real ugly, like fumbles and penalties.

I remember in 2008, we had just beaten Louisiana State University, 27–21, our first victory at Alabama over his former employer and my alma mater, the school where I got hired to work for him, not to mention that the win broke the Crimson Tide's five-game losing streak to the Tigers. You might think he would be loving up the players, but Coach went nuts on the team over either the bad or the ugly. Afterward, a player came to me and said, "You would think we were 0–10 instead of 10–0."

"He doesn't look at it that way," I said. "You're better than that. We could have executed better. He doesn't stand for those penalties. This is not who we are."

Under Coach Saban, the standard is the standard, regardless of what the scoreboard says. That's another reason not to look at the scoreboard. It doesn't matter.

There's nothing magical or hidden about the definition of effort. I can't coach it. No one can. Effort is a choice. We all have to walk through the door with effort. It means showing up every day and giving all that you have, even when you don't feel like you have anything.

Playing college football is a full-time job. The NCAA has tried to put time limits on what coaches may demand of their players, and I suppose it's a good thing that the rules are in place. But the best players ignore the rules anyway. Some guys have motors that never shut down. They are built different mentally. Coaches call them "dogs," as in, "work like a dog."

Dont'a Hightower played linebacker on our first two national championship teams at Alabama. "Guys didn't have a problem embracing the hard work, embracing the suck," Dont'a said. "You'd think, 'I guess it's going to suck now.' But do you want to run around and giggle and get your ass kicked on Saturday? Or do you want to bleed and be bruised up now and have fun kicking their ass on Saturday? That was our mindset."

If you're building a team, you want a player like DeVonta Smith, because he lifts all boats. We had a wide receiver room that included Smitty, Jerry Jeudy, Jaylen Waddle and Henry Ruggs III, all four picked in the top fifteen of their respective NFL drafts. They all made each other better, but I promise you that the other three would not have reached the heights they reached without DeVonta. And he was the least talented of the four of them.

Just the fact that we signed DeVonta as a 157-pound wide receiver should tell you something about him. Coach Saban had height and weight standards for recruits at each position, standards that we ignored in Smitty's case. But we ignored them only because we lost a wide receiver to Georgia, who had backed off Smitty because he was too little. We looked at our board. Smitty was the highest-rated guy. We took a chance. It worked out pretty well. He won the 2020 Heisman Trophy. He won it because he is built differently above the neck.

The thing about recruits is you can't know the size of their motor until they walk into your weight room. Players like Mark Barron, Julio Jones, Minkah Fitzpatrick, and Vinnie Sunseri showed up and outworked everybody at the platform. I only had Will Anderson Jr. for my last two months at Alabama. He came in as a four-star recruit without a lot of publicity. In those few weeks, he changed the work ethic of the linebackers.

Effort, more than any of the other DNA traits, is completely up to the individual. Effort doesn't depend on fast-twitch muscles or any of the other gifts that God provides these kids. I don't know if it's the most powerful of the traits. But it can cover up a lot of mistakes.

You make that effort not just on the field but in the classroom. You make the effort to work hard, yes, but you make the effort to treat people the right way. I know the effort it takes to take notes in class.

YOUR ORGANIZATION'S DNA

I know the effort it takes to pay attention. But we taught the players that the same rules should apply to all aspects of their lives. Make the effort to say hello to the man or woman cleaning the football building. Does that really take much?

Few people on the outside understand how Coach Saban personified effort. He's in his second season of retirement, and he remains a busy man. People thought he walked into the building with his phone to his ear so that he wouldn't have to talk to anyone. Baloney. That's how scheduled he was. We had a staff meeting at 7:30 a.m. He'd have a call with, say, a motivational expert such as Kevin Elko or Lonny Rosen scheduled at 7:25. Whoever Coach had on the line had his full attention on their conversation while he drove into the office. If it ran a little late, then the staff just waited a couple of minutes. He's driving in, talking to someone to get the appropriate psyche for his players.

Coach didn't just dial up a pep talk out of some coaching clinic. He put a lot of importance on his messaging to the players. That was crucial. He ran it by me. He ran it by the staff. He did so to get his reps on his messaging, which, if you think about it, is really cool. By the time he got to the team, he had removed some things and added others, all because he had gotten input. He set the tempo for the week. After he got his third rep with the players, he had his message perfected for the media.

He would call me up to his office. I was not afraid to tell him when I didn't think the players would understand his point. I could give him honest feedback, without fear of losing my job. I don't know why I became that guy. Maybe because I was with the players a lot. I had a good read on them, and sometimes afterward I would think, *I shouldn't have said that*, but he took the information and did it his way. If I had a suggestion, he decided whether he would do it or not. He listened to it, marinated in it, and then decided.

Originally, he bounced ideas off me for his Friday talk to the team. The Friday talk would be motivational, inspirational, and it's funny how often those talks of his gravitated toward toughness. Those were the ones that he and I just absolutely loved. If we had to play somebody twice, we always used Muhammad Ali beating Joe Frazier a second time. If I knew he planned to use that, I'd show the video of the "Thrilla in Manila" from 1975 in the weight room that week. Another favorite fight of his took place in 1980, when Sugar Ray Leonard made Roberto Duran say "No mas." Coach Saban was a fan of making your opponent quit.

Coach actually had a lot of respect for Duran. He won one fight where his opponent kept hitting him with his left hook. It didn't look like it had any effect on Duran. After he won, Duran said something to the effect that if he had been hit with one more left hook, he would have been out cold. His opponent lost the fight because he stopped throwing it. He stopped throwing it because Duran didn't show weakness. Coach told the team, "You're going to take a hit. How you respond is more important than taking the hit."

Toughness is not what young players think it is. It's not just beating the hell out of the guy across the line. That's why I talked about commitment and discipline before I got to toughness. The definition of toughness is not merely physical. You've got to be mentally tough, on and off the field.

Being committed to the process and having discipline and effort to do it is going to be tough.

Being able to not look at the scoreboard is going to be tough.

Being able to not talk back to coaches will be tough.

Not ever talking to an official will be tough.

Or responding to provocation from an opponent. You don't respond to shenanigans on the field or off. Especially off. As big, physical men, football players can be targets on the college social scene. Alcohol creates a lot of tough guys. We made it clear to our players that in a bar, you don't respond. In the real world, you don't respond. Sit on your hands. No one's ever gotten arrested sitting on their hands. If the cops get involved, and you sit on the curb, on your hands, you will not have to worry about a thing.

Pride is a powerful trait for any organization. Take how you dress. Alabama wears crimson at home, white on the road, crimson helmets. Period. Those are powerful symbols. I know that corporate dress codes have taken a beating since COVID. I hear the coat and tie are making a comeback. There is something powerful about pride in your appearance, pride in your performance, pride in who you're becoming, pride in the result of all your effort. Pride, to me, delivers your self-confidence. They go hand in hand. I've been committed to the program. I've had discipline. I put in a lot of effort. It's been tough. Now I have the confidence to execute.

Pride is also wearing a coat and tie on the road. You make the effort to present yourself in a professional manner. Pride is cleaning the locker room and the weight room. Pride is keeping your stuff clean and leaving the locker room better than you found it. And we didn't let it become a case of the older guys telling the younger guys to pick up their stuff. We made it clear from the first day a freshman arrived on campus that every single player had accountability. Pride in doing the right thing, pride in tucking in your shirt, pride in taking your hat off in buildings, pride in doing what you're supposed to do. Pride in your performance. Pride in your commitment to excellence.

Pride is the manifestation of the other four DNA traits. I can't imagine any leader wanting a trait more than pride because of what it represents.

We always used the illustration of the All Blacks, the fearsome national rugby team of New Zealand, and how they remain so successful. I remember hearing that their captains cleaned up the locker room after the team left. They took pride in doing the haka, the Māori ceremonial dance. They took pride in the way that those all-black uniforms look.

One warning: If you're not careful, pride can turn into a bit of a swagger. It's got to be pride in your DNA traits, not pride in self. That is an important lesson, especially with young athletes who are shoved onto a pedestal whether they're ready or not. Celebrity at a young age, when you don't expect it and can't understand what it really means, is tough. It can become another form of addiction, another high.

Listen, I'm not a college athlete, and I got sucked in by the look-at-me high. My love language is affirmations. Cissy tried to keep me humble. She is always trying to keep my hat size in single digits. Cissy would say, "No, I don't think you need to hear that. You hear that enough."

I continued to hear all the "Coach Yeah!" love as I sunk deeper and deeper into addiction. My ego kept telling me that I could and should be a head coach. I know better now. My ego got stomped down to where you could slide it under the door.

That's why, when I got the phone call from Joseph Brown, the vice-president of the University

YOUR ORGANIZATION'S DNA

of West Alabama board of trustees, I thought he wanted me to speak on campus about my addiction journey. When he told me why he called, I said, "Are you sure you're talking to the right person? I've never been a head coach before. Why would you seek me out?"

He told me that in 2012, he had brought a leadership group to the Paul W. Bryant Conference Center across the street from the Alabama football building. They sat among five hundred people and listened to the keynote speaker—me. He said I had the entire building ready to sprint across the street and suit up for two-a-days.

If I'm ever in a position to hire that guy as my head coach, he thought, *I'm hiring him.*

Then he said, "This is the call."

I remember the speech, which is interesting, because I did so many of them. I remember the gist of my talk, what got five hundred people so fired up: I spoke about these five DNA traits.

Once you have established your DNA traits, and you have a corporate culture, you can apply those traits to the task in front of you. That's the best way I can define a mission statement. Disney does whatever it has to do to make Disneyland the "Happiest Place on Earth." I think of the days when FedEx used the slogan "When It Absolutely, Positively Has to Be There Overnight." A mission statement identifies what you plan to do. It identifies it not only to the people inside your doors but also to the whole big world out there. In one statement, FedEx explained to its customers what the company did, what the task demanded of FedEx's employees, and how hard they intended to work to make it happen.

The trick is to find the mission statement that everybody in your building understands and can get behind. That means you have to find the right words. At Alabama, according to Coach Saban, we were "A Team Nobody Wants to Play." In 2022, at Georgia, we used "Burn the Boats." Drew Brannon, the program's sports psychologist, came up with that. Burn the Boats, as in there's no going back. It worked pretty well. Not only did we beat Alabama in the national championship game, 33–18, we beat them by dominating the fourth quarter. Alabama, the original fourth-quarter team.

YOUR ORGANIZATION'S DNA

Football teams love "Hold the Rope." I'm pretty sure every high school team in America has used it. Greg Schiano used "Keep Chopping Wood" at Rutgers. P.J. Fleck, at Western Michigan and at Minnesota, has become known for "Row the Boat." All three of them deliver the same message. You have to do your job, over and over, even when you're tired, even when you're sore, even when you would rather be doing anything else. You have to outwork the team across the line.

Your mission statement is similar to positive self-talk, which I will discuss in chapter 10, but a mission statement exists on a larger scale. Your mission statement is a rallying cry for the whole organization. It is a product of establishing the culture. It points your people in the right direction and frames the identity that they have worked so hard to establish through adhering to your DNA traits. When your people know who they are, they will know what they must do. That's how you win.

THREE

BEGINNINGS

My mom, Susan Cochran, a teacher, worked in a nonprofit called Jobs for America's Graduates at a New Orleans high school. She worked with the kids who had no chance to go to college. She always brought in the military recruiters. She brought in all kinds of recruiters. I don't know why, but her work instilled in me that there's a future for these kids, and what you teach them is going to help them. I think, quite simply, what I saw is how much Mom cared. That's where my career started, too.

My dad, Bill Cochran, told me that from the age of ten I said I intended to become a coach and I wanted to make a difference in people's lives. On my high school team, Coach Curtis held us to high standards and did not accept any effort that failed to meet them. Playing for Coach Curtis might explain why I clicked with Coach Saban. Ya think?

I loved the weight room. Loved being part of a team. But my talent on the field peaked in high school. Luckily for me, I paid attention in school. I graduated with a GPA high enough that I qualified for the in-state TOPS Scholarship. I went to LSU on the state's dime and wanted to pursue a physical therapy career. My older brothers, Billy and Brian, both became physical therapists. I watched them make good money, so I decided to become one, too. In those days, you didn't have to get an undergraduate degree to go to PT school. You needed only thirty-six hours on your college transcript. I got my thirty-six hours, I was a sophomore, it was 1998, and I planned to go to a PT school in Amsterdam that is accredited in the United States. It would have cost me only $20,000 for three years.

I was all set to take out a big loan, and my dad said no.

What do you mean, no? At that time, I worked as a bartender. I cut grass. I went to class. Three jobs, two of them paying me so that I could cover my bills, and I had found a clear path to a good-paying job. And Dad stopped me.

"You've said you were going to coach ever since you were a kid, and you haven't even tried," he said. Mom didn't share his vision. The high school teacher in her said to me, "I don't want you to be a broke, drunk high school coach."

My dad made a good living as an accountant. But let's face it, no one grows up dreaming of being an accountant. He reminded me of my dream.

"Try," he said. "Just go and try."

In theory, good advice. In reality, I didn't have a car, so I went to the high school I could walk to, University High Laboratory School on the LSU campus. I set up an interview with the head coach, Wayne Williams, to be a volunteer coach. I put on a sport coat and tie and walked over to see him. I had to walk through the weight room to get to Coach Williams's office. I stepped inside, and within ten seconds, I knew: *This is what I am meant to do.* I never made it to his office.

I saw a guy struggling on one of the machines. "Can I help you with that?" I asked.

"Heck, yeah," he said.

SKULL SESSION

The sport coat came off. The tie came off. I was just enthralled by the players. They listened to what I said! They listened like they were eager. I started coaching one player, and then everybody started asking me questions, and I just felt at home. So I forgot about the interview. Coach Williams came walking in, and he said, "I'm waiting to see this college guy. He's supposed to be interviewing for a job. I can't find him. I guess he didn't show up."

"Oh man, that's me," I said. "I'm sorry. My fault."

"What are you doing?" he asked.

"These kids didn't know what they were doing," I said. "I just started helping them."

Coach Williams looked at me. "Well," he said, "you got the job."

I became the special teams coach, the linebackers coach, the running backs coach, and the weight room guy. I made $200 a month, and I was happy as can be, because I didn't have to work at the bar and I didn't have to go cut grass in the morning. I just dove in. We ran eight punt fakes in two years, and we converted every one of them. It was unbelievable. Coach Williams would look at me and ask, "You got something?"

"We'll see," I'd say. "I called it, but it's a call. If it's open, they're gonna take it.'" And it worked. It was crazy. I fell in love.

I studied abroad for eight months at Deakin University in Melbourne, Australia. I turned twenty-one while I was over there, and when I came back, LSU had hired Nick Saban, taking him away from Michigan State. Coach Saban hired my high school strength coach, Tommy Moffitt, who had been at the University of Miami. I reached out to Coach Moffitt. "Hey," I said, "I'm coaching at the high school on campus, but when the season ends, can I come work for you?"

"You can come now," he said. "I need all the help I can get."

Coach Moffitt knew I knew the technique that he taught. I just started volunteering for him. There went my $200 a month. But I didn't pull out my lawn mower. I saw the staff that he had, and I figured out some of his guys would graduate. I thought, *If I can hurry up my studies and time it right, I'll be his next graduate assistant.* I changed my degree from physical therapy to sports studies, an easier degree. That got me to a diploma faster, which got me $800 a month for being a GA.

Eventually I got my master's in sports management, paid for by LSU.

As a GA, I became head strength coach for gymnastics, swimming, and diving. I helped out with baseball, basketball, and, of course, with football. But when I took the job, I told Coach Moffitt the only way I would leave the high school is if I could help out the football coaches on the field, too. Michael Haywood and Derek Dooley handled the special teams, and they didn't have a GA dedicated to them, so I helped them. That's how I began to really learn the kicking game.

I also helped out the scout team, and that's how I got to know Coach Saban. Being on the field also helped me get my nickname. I had a high school teammate, a gigantic defensive lineman named Tony Mitchell. Anytime he got a sack, he would yell, "Yeah! Yeah! Yeah!" Fast-forward to LSU, where we had a linebacker named Jason Ledoux. He looked so much like Tony that he got me to thinking about Tony, and I started saying "Yeah! Yeah! Yeah!" Only I added a couple of more *Yeahs!* and yelled them without so much as a split second between them. It became my tag, an outpouring of love and excitement, and it's much better than dropping a load of F bombs.

At Alabama, we had a defensive back named Ha Ha Clinton-Dix. He became an All-American for us, played seven seasons in the NFL, and now is back at Alabama as director of player development for coach Kalen DeBoer. In the middle of our Fourth Quarter conditioning drills, he kind of blew me off, made it clear that he had an issue. Afterward, I asked him what was going on, and he said, "Man, when you start cussing, I just block you out. It just doesn't feel right." That really hit me. The next day, I told the team, "You're gonna hear some funny words out of my mouth, but I'm really working on this. You have your goals, your Skull Session for the week. Mine is to stop cussing." I'm still trying.

As strength coach for the women's swimming team, I met an outstanding breaststroker named Cissy Schepens. She swam at LSU for two years, swam at the 2000 Olympic Trials, and transferred to Georgia, which won the 2001 NCAA title. LSU offered her a full scholarship to come back—sounds almost like the transfer portal nowadays, doesn't it?—and she came back. That's when I became her

SKULL SESSION

strength coach in name only. I couldn't coach her because of a conflict of interest. My coaching conflicted with my interest—I had the hots for her.

I knew I couldn't act on it. I got the job because a guy before me had crossed the line with one of the female athletes. I had no intention of getting fired. I didn't think she would really be into me anyway. I thought she was way out of my league.

Cissy didn't like the weight room. She and her breaststrokers would come over and do some work with medicine balls. One day we got some snow in Baton Rouge, and she and her crew didn't show up for workout. I called her and asked where they were.

"It's snowing!" she said.

I made them clean the weight room the next day.

I really did try to steer clear of Cissy. I'd see her when the breaststrokers ran stadium stairs. I was loud even then, saying stuff largely for entertainment value. I'd yell, "If you're scared, go to church, but this time I'm not driving." The breaststrokers made T-shirts with that saying on them and wore them to the weight room. Cissy told me later that I made workouts fun, an important criterion for

BEGINNINGS

athletes whose choice of variety is to stare at the bottom of the pool or at the end of the pool.

The women's swimming season ended on March 22, the last day of the NCAA championships. That night, as the team bus made its way back to campus, I called her. It was close to midnight, but I had waited long enough. I met her at the bus. We walked over to a bar and hung out until 2 a.m. And that was pretty much that. We got married two years later, in August 2005.

By then, I worked for the New Orleans Hornets (now the Pelicans) of the NBA as an assistant strength coach. I'd like to tell you that they heard about my work for Coach Moffitt and recruited me. What happened is that someone from the Hornets called the LSU weight room and I answered the phone.

"Is there someone there who would be interested in being an assistant strength coach for the Hornets?" he asked.

Yes, there was. They offered me $50,000 a year. My reaction: *Really? That means I can propose to Cissy. Let's go!*

On our honeymoon, we took a cruise down to Cozumel. As we left, the captain mentioned

SKULL SESSION

something about a big storm entering the Gulf of Mexico but not to worry. We would beat it to New Orleans.

The big storm's name was Katrina. When we got back in open water, waves as high as thirteen feet hit the ship. We had a cabin on the eighth floor. I opened the window and leaned out. One of those big waves slammed into the ship and bounced up the side, and I got drenched.

When the captain contacted the port of New Orleans to tell them he intended to drop off 2,500 passengers as scheduled, they said, *The hell you are. You gotta go to Galveston.* We didn't see New Orleans for two weeks. Actually, I never worked there again. The Hornets played in Oklahoma City for the next two seasons.

The Hornets didn't win much during my time there, but I got great experience. In the second week of January 2007, we had hit a rut and lost eight of nine games. We were in Atlanta to play the Hawks. I got a phone call from Bo Davis, who had worked with me as a strength coach at LSU and then gone with Coach Saban to the Dolphins as a defensive line coach. A week earlier, Alabama had rocked the college football world by hiring Saban as head coach. Bo went with him to Tuscaloosa.

Bo reached out and said, "Nick's gonna call you." He didn't say what about, but that told me that Tommy Moffitt wasn't leaving LSU for Alabama.

The first thing Nick said, "I don't know if you know, but I took the job at Alabama."

"No, I haven't seen anything on ESPN," I said. "I don't see that the people in Miami are going to kill you. I have no idea, Coach, no, not at all."

He didn't laugh. Note to self: Coach isn't into sarcasm.

He told me he wanted to interview me to be the head strength coach. I couldn't say yes fast enough. He said, "Be here in the morning."

"Coach, all I got with me are velour Hornets warm-up suits. Can I go back to Oklahoma City and get my clothes?"

"I'm not hiring you to be a fucking banker," Saban barked. "Be here in the morning."

I rented a car and started driving. My first stop, a Walmart open late at night. I bought a blazer, slacks, shirt, and tie. He interviewed me and offered me $120,000, more than double my salary, to be head strength coach at Alabama.

Coach said, "Shake my hand."

I shook it.

"You're not gonna go back to the Hornets and them offer you a bunch of money?" Coach asked.

"No, we're good," I said.

Of course, when I went back to the Hornets, that's exactly what they did. They offered me new duties and a lot more money. I remained polite, but I was gone. Why did it take somebody else offering me money for them to want to pay me what I was worth?

By the way, that Walmart blazer became a lucky charm. In 2006, the Alabama kicker, a freshman named Leigh Tiffin, had a nightmarish game at Arkansas. He missed three field goals, one of them in overtime, then missed an extra point in overtime, and Arkansas won, 24–23.

A year later, our first season, we played Arkansas in our third game. Early that week, Brian Selman, the long snapper, told me that Leigh already had started freaking out and that I needed to love him up. I wore the Walmart blazer to the game, showed Leigh how awesome I looked in it. I let him know the Walmart blazer is my lucky blazer, and that he would never miss against Arkansas again. Leigh made two field goals against the Hogs, one in the fourth quarter after we had blown a three-touchdown lead, and we came back to win by...3 points.

By 2009, the year we won our first national championship at Alabama, Leigh Tiffin became an All-American. My Walmart blazer continued to hold a place of honor in my wardrobe, until we went on a road trip one season and one of the players had forgotten to pack a jacket. I lent it to him so that he wouldn't get in trouble, and I never saw it again.

FOUR

COACH SABAN

In more ways than I can explain, my life changed because I had the opportunity to work for and to learn from Nick Saban. He taught me how to work. He taught me how to win. I look back over twenty-five years—I can't believe it's been that long—and see how far I have come because he believed in me. I know I sound like a Celine Dion song, but that doesn't make it less true.

Not to mention you don't want to hear me sing.

In one sense, both of us won our bets on one another. I didn't go to work for Coach Saban at LSU with a premonition that he would become the GOAT. I mainly wanted a job doing something I liked. Coach didn't know I would transform into not only a strength coach but an expert in motivation, a guy he could trust to have his finger on the pulse of the locker room.

We had a good thing going for a very long time. We certainly didn't start that way.

At the end of my first day in Tuscaloosa, Coach Saban called me into his office. I had worked out five groups of players that day. Coach had come down at one point to watch them work. In my memory, that's the only time he ever set foot in the weight room.

"I don't see any players," he said in his office. He didn't mean the weight room was empty. He meant none of the guys he watched work out looked like they had enough physical ability to play for him.

"I haven't seen one," I said. "Not one."

Saban based his judgment on thirty-five years of coaching experience. All I had to judge by was the only college program I had been around—Saban's LSU teams a few years before, one of which won the national championship. NFL teams drafted seventeen players who played for the 2003 national champions, seven of them in the first two rounds. We had studs. What I saw among the players in my Alabama workouts did not compare.

"What about Andre Smith?" Coach asked.

"I don't know who that is," I said.

"He's an offensive lineman. He's really good, really talented."

"If it's the guy I think it is," I said, "he weighs about four hundred pounds."

"That's him."

Andre, at the outset, was not very interested in what we had to offer. He wasn't an outlier, either. We met up with skepticism, apprehension, chips on shoulders, fear. There was enthusiasm, too. We explained to all of the players that we didn't automatically dislike them. We didn't automatically like them. We had our standard, and they would have to meet it. Greg McElroy, our quarterback who's now a star on ESPN, remembers how much leadership we had. "If Coach Cochran would have had a bunch of rock heads," Greg said, "it would have been a much tougher transition for everybody. But he had guys who really wanted to be great."

Maybe so, but they weren't the only ones looking to prove themselves. I was in charge for the first time in my young career. I used the exact blueprint that Coach Moffitt had taught me. I was too scared to do any trial and error. Why would I change anything? I knew it worked, not to mention that it was also the only thing I knew. Coach Saban also surrounded me with assistants and player development guys who had a lot of coaching experience or had played the game at a high level, guys like Jeremy Pruitt, Willie Carl Martin, Rob Sale, and, in my second year, Freddie Roach, who's now the assistant head coach at Alabama. "It was about surrounding the players with people who had played," Freddie said, "guys who could either help motivate the players or help push them to become bigger and better than they even thought they could be."

The other side of my job, getting into my players' heads, learning how to motivate them, I believed I would be able to figure out. The way I looked at it, by definition I had to play good cop to Coach Saban's bad cop. It was a role that I could play more easily, because at twenty-seven years old, I wasn't that much older than they were. A strength coach is there every day, and I tried to be consistent every day.

I learned how to motivate with the help of experts such as Lonny Rosen, Trevor Moawad, and Kevin Elko. I would search the internet for others. I'd call them, listen to their approaches to reaching players and motivating them to be the best they can be, and if I thought it would work, I would bring them into Tuscaloosa.

But let's not get ahead of ourselves.

The first two years, I constantly got coached by Coach Saban. He believed in me enough to hire me, but he also knew I was in my twenties and I would make more than my share of mistakes. One of the biggest happened early in the 2008 season, our second. We had a road trip to No. 3 Georgia that week. We were No. 8, a ranking we earned on the strength of Coach Saban's resume and a season-opening win against what proved to be a very overranked Clemson team.

Georgia had announced that the game Saturday night at Sanford Stadium would be a blackout. They asked all their fans to leave their red clothes at home and wear black. At Wednesday practice, during what we called flex period—basically, warm-up time—I put on my motivational hat. I wandered through the lines of players, talking, clapping, yelling, getting them hyped up for a physical practice in preparation for a physical game.

"They're wearing black," I yelled, "because they're going to a fucking funeral!"

SKULL SESSION

If I had thought at all before I said it, I would have realized that Coach allowed the media into practice for warm-ups, so the TV stations could have some video for the evening news. I'm yelling, the players are yelling, and it's usually just a lot of noise. But someone's microphone picked up me being witty.

Yep, my little joke ran on the news, and in about the time it takes to warm up a printer, ended up posted everywhere the Georgia team could see it. The next day, Jeff Purinton, Coach's media guy (now the athletic director at Arkansas State), let Coach know that his young dumbass of a strength coach had given Georgia some unrequested motivation. You might ask why Jeff told Coach, and the answer is simple: Coach hated surprises. The media would be asking him about it after practice.

I'll never forget. I was with our big defensive lineman, Terrence Cody, who was doing some extra running to try to lose weight.

"Coach wants to see you," Jeff said.

Now I felt like the one going to a fucking funeral.

As I walked up there, I decided not to just sit there and take it. I decided to throw the first punch—at myself. I went into Coach's office and started cussing myself out.

"I can't believe it, Coach!" I started. "I can't believe that came out of my mouth at the wrong time. I'm such an idiot! I'm just giving Georgia stuff for their bulletin board. They've got it up all over the place. I mean, this is the absolute worst thing I ever wanted to have happen."

I fell on the grenade, and it saved my life.

"It's okay, Cochran! It's okay," Coach said. "I hate that it happened, but it's not your fault. We're gonna get on the media about it."

Then Coach turned on Jeff and began berating him about the story getting out there. He chewed Jeff up and down. Jeff said later he learned a valuable lesson. If he screwed up, he went into Coach's office and chewed himself out, too. We all learned the best thing to do with Coach was to own the mistake. Eventually, when Coach got mad about something, and I got madder than he did, he would say, "Stop taking the blame for everything! I know this is not your fault! Just tell me how this came about?"

"It's my fault, Coach, I shouldn't have done it."

"No, you're full of shit! Tell me the truth."

SKULL SESSION

I devised my strategy in order to get through whatever lit Coach's fuse because I believed we had more important things to do, like win football games. But Coach taught me an important lesson about achieving a goal and about time management. He focused on finding the mistake and correcting it. He didn't want to know why I did what I did. He didn't want to spend time on excuses, on why I just knew my way was better, or how I had car trouble, or what meeting ran long and made me late for his meeting. One reason that Coach loved Jalen Hurts is that Jalen wouldn't try to explain why he made the wrong decision with the ball. He accepted the coaching and promised to do better.

For the record, that bulletin-board funeral at Georgia? The players knew that Coach wasn't happy with me. They told me, "Don't worry. We got your back." We led 31–0 at the half.

After a couple of years, Coach began to trust me enough that he didn't coach me all the time. He knew that I had the ear of the players. More important, he knew that I had the heartbeat of the team.

Coach didn't hire me for this particular task, but I got to know the players well enough that I would keep him apprised of the issues that they faced. It's easy to forget, amid all the hype of a highly ranked college football team, that those stars are still young people with the problems that young people face. I thought it my duty to help the players navigate their interactions with Coach. I would decide whether some news about the player should come to Coach from the kid himself or if I should handle it. This kid has these academic issues, that kid pledged a fraternity, and the other one has a child on the way. Coach would be mad about a player's behavior, and I would try to get in front of it, take the angry response, so that when the player showed up in Coach's office, Coach would have moved past ass-chewing and into consolation.

Our relationship evolved as the years went forward. I became much more of a sounding board for him, especially once Kirby left for Georgia after the 2015 season. During the season, Coach and I met on Sunday nights for a half hour or so to discuss the emotional state of the team and how we would motivate the players in the week to come. I learned that the best way to motivate them was to make the game personal, come up with some reason that they had a stake in it. Make it personal, and the players always will take the extra step to prepare. They'll watch more film, do one more rep, perform extra drills.

Of course, some weeks, I didn't have to work very hard. I never had to come up with a gimmick for LSU. There was never a better week to be around Coach Saban than LSU Week. He would have a smile on his face all week, going out of his way to look calm and really confident. He understood how important this game had become to our players. We had a lot of kids from Louisiana—and one strength coach. About 10 percent of our roster came from Louisiana, including stars such as DeVonta Smith, Eddie Lacy, Christian Harris, Tim Williams, Landon Collins, Cam Robinson, and Dylan Moses—and that's not close to being everyone. It was personal for them. Either they didn't get recruited by LSU or they chose Alabama over LSU. As a Louisiana native, I felt the same way. We'd always say, "I can't go back home if we lose this game. I can't go visit my family, because I'm gonna hear it from everybody in the neighborhood."

That's why every time we played them, it was a war. But we had a lot of success. In my thirteen seasons at Alabama, we went 10–4 against LSU. All four of those losses were by one score, and two of the LSU teams that beat us won the national championship.

Auburn games certainly held our attention. We all know that's a 365-day rivalry in the state of Alabama, and although we dominated the Iron Bowl in my thirteen seasons (eight wins, by an average of 24 points) we lost two gut-punch games. We blew a 24-point lead and lost by a point in 2010, and in 2013, we lost the Kick Six, the craziest set of circumstances that caused a loss that ever occurred on a football field. If you don't know what I'm talking about, look it up. I can't go through them again. Anyway, those two losses made sure we never lost our focus against Auburn.

Coach also would adopt an upbeat attitude for the season opener because we always played a nationally prominent opponent, a Clemson or Wisconsin or USC or Michigan, in a game arranged for TV. We would train so hard leading up to the season that when we went into the first game, it didn't matter who we were playing, we played well. The players had heard us challenge their ability for eight months. They went into the opener kind of fearful

SKULL SESSION

that they would get their butts whipped. Think about it—new starters were guys who had always filled in, who didn't have the confidence that comes with experience.

I remember the 2012 opener against Michigan. We built up the ability of the Michigan secondary so high that after the game, Amari Cooper told me, "Man, I thought Michigan was gonna kill us." We won, 41–14. We ran the ball forty-two times and threw only twenty-one passes. Amari caught one pass. He never balked. He wanted to win.

At the other end of the spectrum were game likes Western Kentucky, Fresno State, the "paycheck opponents" who would submit themselves to a beatdown at Bryant-Denny Stadium for a considerable fee. Those weeks, Coach would be the worst to be around. He made sure that every detail mattered because otherwise, the players wouldn't pay attention. We all knew he would get on everyone's ass. That was his default method. Those weeks in particular, we made it our mission to take care of the details. We would tell the players over and over, "We're not there yet." The older they got, the more they would figure out that under Coach Saban, no team ever arrives "there."

In his later seasons, when we battled Georgia for national honors on a yearly basis, Coach would try to take that LSU-like upbeat approach to play the Dawgs. By Thursday, he would regret it. His nerves would get to him, and he would throw a fit. I would pick up his concerns and challenge the players: "Y'all aren't taking these guys seriously!" It usually worked out. We beat Georgia twice in the SEC Championship Game and once for the national title.

My favorite story about how Coach got us ready happened on the next-to-last weekend of the 2011 season. We had lost a 9–6 overtime heartbreaker to LSU at home.

We had all the motivation in the world to keep playing hard because we held out hope that we would get the chance to play LSU again for the national championship. But we needed help. Remember, in the days of the BCS, only two teams went to the playoff. That meant two teams ahead of us had to lose. One week, No. 1 Baylor got smoked at home by Kansas State. We moved up to No. 3. On the next Friday night, the Friday before Thanksgiving, No. 2 Oklahoma State lost at Iowa State in double overtime, 37–31.

SKULL SESSION

We had Georgia Southern, the annual paycheck opponent, the week before Auburn. Coach Saban had been tough that week. When Oklahoma State lost, I thought the second floor of the team hotel would cave straight down to the lobby. They started jumping up and down, screaming and carrying on. The way that Dont'a Hightower, a senior linebacker that season, put it, "We went buck fucking stupid in there. We went crazy for, like, twenty minutes. Everyone busted out into the hallways, jumping, running up and down. That was the problem. Everybody knew we were supposed to be in bed. It was after curfew. We had an early-morning game the next day. We were running around, going crazy. It was wild."

The assistant coaches didn't so much as tap the brakes on our reaction, either. All of us celebrated.

We got into the staff meeting on Saturday morning, gameday, all of us so upbeat. You would think we would know better. Oh my God, that had to be the worst attitude we could have taken. Coach Saban came into the meeting and went off. He went nuts, absolutely crazy on us. He told us we weren't in the playoff yet, and that we were taking our eye off the ball. You name it, he accused us of it.

He got through chewing us out, and as we all filed out of the room, chastened, he grabbed me. At that point, I was terrified of him because he was so pissed.

"I'm gonna grab the team before the pregame meal and talk to them," he said.

"You should give them exactly what you just gave us," I told him. "They need it. They celebrated last night."

Sure enough, right after the team prayer, he unloaded on them.

When we got to the stadium, I came out on the field with the players for the pregame stretch and warm-up, and I saw Coach's uncle, Sid Popovich, who came to a lot of games. Uncle Sid is on the sideline with us, in the locker room with us. I saw him on the sideline, eating a snack or something. And I just said, "What's up, Uncle Sid?"

"Scott, did you see that Oklahoma State game last night?"

"Yeah, I saw it," I said. "The players are excited. They got a chance to get to the championship game."

Uncle Sid said, "Man, you should have seen Coach last night. After Oklahoma State lost, oh my

God! He was so happy! He was standing on his chair; he was dancing, I've never seen him so happy! It was the best. He was in such a good mood. It was awesome, man. He left the house this morning in a good mood. I mean, I had coffee with him before he left. He was in such a good mood."

"You gotta be kidding me," I said.

"No!" he said. "It was the best."

I looked at him.

"Uncle Sid," I said. "Don't tell a *soul* that that happened."

Coach always had a great barometer for the players. So many times he said or did the complete opposite of what you felt. That day, he did the complete opposite of what *he* felt. Turned out he was right. Our defense never really tuned in that day. Georgia Southern rushed for 302 yards. They never got closer than ten points to us, though, and we won, 45–21.

Jeff Purinton called that Coach Saban's perfect day: We won, and he got to yell at us. I'm pretty sure Coach never berated himself for how he reacted, though.

FIVE

SMART GOALS

I had the good luck to be a college sophomore when I figured out what I wanted to do for the rest of my life. That's rare. I fell in love with something. As I said, I wouldn't have done it without my dad reminding me of my childhood dream of becoming a coach. As a sophomore, with two older brothers who had started their careers, I knew enough to worry about whether I could coach and make a living. My dad had an answer for that, too, an answer that only comes with experience. If I followed my dream, he said, "you will find a way to make money." I kept the main thing the main thing. I worked, but I had fun. And I did find a way to make money.

SKULL SESSION

I always have been a goal-setter. My dad gave me the boost to try coaching, and my mom taught me how important it is to have a carrot dangling in front of you. But I didn't harness the true power of goals until I gave them direction. We called them SMART goals: *specific, measurable, accountable, reachable* goals in a defined *time frame*. For you and the people working with you, making your goals SMART will turbocharge them and allow your organization to maintain its focus for a long time.

To be honest, my discovery of the power of goals actually happened because I saw someone else had written his goals down. I walked past Amari Cooper's locker one day his junior year at Alabama, 2014, the year he won SEC Offensive Player of the Year *as a wide receiver*. That's in italics because that's a tough position from which to dominate a game, much less a season. In my lifetime only three wideouts have won a Player of the Year Award in the SEC. I got to coach two of them. DeVonta Smith won the award, as well as the Heisman Trophy, in 2020, the season after I left for Georgia.

Amari had written down his goals and posted them on his locker, where he saw them every day. He wanted to catch this many passes, score this many touchdowns, get this many yards, become an All-American, and win the Heisman. He listed them out, 1-2-3-4-5. He made them specific. He didn't write, "I want to be the next Jerry Rice!" Amari made his goals measurable in the official currency of wide receivers: receptions, yards, touchdowns, honors. By writing them down, Amari made himself accountable. He didn't have to hang them where everyone, including me, could read them, but that made him even more accountable. That may have been a measure of his confidence, or it may have been Amari pushing in all his chips on himself.

Whatever the reason, Amari stood there looking at them as if he were in a museum studying a Rembrandt. When I saw him, I thought, "There's got to be a way to double down on that." I learned from Amari to give our players a goals sheet. I asked them to list three daily goals on a grid that had check marks for each day of the week. Below that, I included a smaller grid on which to list weekly goals. At the bottom, I asked them to list major, big-picture goals, like first-round draft pick, All-American, 4.0 GPA.

For a parent, the daily goals might be thirty minutes of exercise, bath time with kids, do the dishes. The weekly goal might be five workouts. Yeah, that's where the idea of reachable goals comes into play. You don't want to make your goal so crazy that you can't reach it. Anytime you make your goals too big, you just throw them away, and they do nothing for you. That's why New Year's resolutions fizzle out before you get to February. They're too big. The key is to find something that you know you're going to do. Everyone in my weight room wanted to squat 500 pounds, but if you walk in there and you're squatting 250, your next goal should be 275. Remember, you're eating an elephant. The best way to eat an elephant is to take one bite at a time.

That's where the last part of the acronym comes in. The time frame may be a week. It may be a day. The point is that you know what you have to do. You're breaking it down to something small, a digestible bite, even if you're eating an elephant. As a result, you feel good about yourself.

It should be self-evident that SMART goals apply to the business world. They apply to anything: football, parenting, you name it. All they take is a little mental discipline and a lot of desire, which are pretty much prerequisites for success.

SMART GOALS

A checklist of goals helps you refocus. Kids today don't know to do checklists. I remember doing checklists forever at their age, like, "These are the ten things I want to do today." I would start with something I already had done so I could have one with a check next to it. That may be like starting a 100-yard sprint on the 10-yard line, but there's nothing wrong with a boost to get you started.

I have benefited from having goals. But I'll give you one warning: You can get into trouble if your goals are there to massage your ego. I fell into that trap at Alabama. I listed my three goals as ten national championships, making a million dollars, and fifty first-rounders in the NFL draft. When I left Georgia, I had won eight national championships, made a ton of money, and had more than fifty first-rounders. And I was a train wreck.

I don't have any regrets. None.

Here is a good place to tell a story that brought me a lot of attention. Not that it should have. It wasn't supposed to be public. In January 2017, Alabama played a national championship rematch against Clemson in Tampa. The Tigers got us, throwing a touchdown with one second left to play to beat us, 35–31. Just an absolutely gutting loss. A few weeks later, as I headed into a meeting with Coach Saban, I came to a full stop. I saw a trophy sitting on a desk in the hallway outside of his office. I asked Linda Leoni, his longtime secretary, "Hey, what is that?"

"That's what they sent us," Linda said, they being the College Football Playoff. It was a runner-up trophy. An award for finishing second. Recognition for not winning.

"What are we doing with it?" I asked.

"I don't know," Linda said. "I don't even think Nick knows we have it. Just take it if you want it."

Did I ever. I put the trophy in my office, where all the players could see it. When one of them walked in after being late for a workout or being late to a class or missing a meeting, I would just point to the trophy and say, "How did that feel? Because your behavior is the type of behavior that gets a participation award."

The trophy served as a great motivational tool. We made the playoff and defeated Clemson, 24–6, in the Sugar Bowl semifinal. The team came back to Tuscaloosa really tired. You'd think that since we beat the national champion, the team that had broken our heart the season before, we would get our energy back. But the game took a toll on us.

SMART GOALS

We needed something. I had some team leaders in my office. I know linebacker Rashaan Evans was one of them. Someone looked at the trophy and said, "What are we doing with that?"

"What do you mean?" I asked. "There's nothing to do with it."

"We just made up for that loss," one of the players said. "We just beat Clemson."

The idea just popped into my head, a way to remind everyone, as we tried to get our minds right to play a very good Georgia team, what we think of second place. I decided to smash the trophy in front of the team.

I thought about doing it when everyone gathered on the practice field, but I worried that the shards of the trophy would bury in the turf and we wouldn't be able to use it. I chose the locker room, which is supposed to be a very safe place. Safe, as in "what happens in the locker room stays in the locker room." No cameras. Except that when I walked into the locker room holding the trophy and a sledgehammer, wide receiver Jerry Jeudy pulled out his phone and started recording a video. On one hand, I don't think he or anyone else knew what I intended to do. On the other, Jerry put two and two together.

SKULL SESSION

To recap, I had (a) a trophy and (b) a sledgehammer. I raised the trophy above my head and slammed it onto the carpet. Pieces went every which way. Then I did my best Gallagher and swung the sledgehammer into the biggest piece like a watermelon.

I have to say, the guys loved it. They got so fired up. The next Monday night, we beat Georgia, the game when Tua Tagovailoa rescued us after halftime. We won our fifth national championship in eight seasons. Add in the championship team at LSU in 2003, and I had won six rings, more than halfway to my career goal of ten. My big-picture goals—the million-dollar income and the fifty first-rounders, too—were insane. It kind of shows you where my ego was. The fact that I got close to reaching all three of them doesn't make them any less insane. Those goals served my ego, the same ego that figured that being so successful, being famous enough to do commercials, being profiled on *60 Minutes*, I would never become addicted to pills. Me? No way! You see my house? See my cars?

That's ego: "Edging God Out," as we learn in recovery. My goals didn't serve me. They became about me. My goals now are very different. They are (1) help others, (2) be the best husband and father I can be, and (3) keep God first. I remind myself that in the Bible, Amos was just a businessman. God made him a prophet. Moses stuttered, but God gave him the power to lead the people. I remind myself that I'm just a strength coach. It's okay if I screw up. It lowers the pressure I put on myself down to a manageable level.

Recovery taught me something else about my SMART goals. Competition is the very definition of measurability and accountability. I think you have to have something in your job where you think, *Shoot, I gotta get that done.* I always thought that drumbeat gave me an edge. I had spent my entire career working at a frantic pace. In 2024, when I didn't coach and I focused on being healthy and getting my AARA foundation on its feet, I found the work gratifying. But I missed competition, the measurable outcome of building a team toward a common goal. The speaking engagements weren't enough.

I'm back to competing now. I'm sure from the outside it looks like a frantic pace, but anyone in the building can see that I'm enjoying it. I'm not in a rush to leave. I get here early. I take time with people. I'm back in competition.

SKULL SESSION

I'll make one more point about accountability. For my work with AARA last year, I had to go to Las Vegas. While there I got to visit Henry Ruggs III, who had been a stud wide receiver for us at Alabama. The Raiders drafted him in the first round of the 2020 NFL draft. In November 2021, after he had started nineteen games in his NFL career, Henry got behind the wheel of his Corvette after a night of drinking and collided with a woman at a high speed, causing her car to burst into flames. Both the woman and her dog died. Henry is serving a sentence of three to ten years for felony DUI causing death and misdemeanor vehicular manslaughter. His career was interrupted and is possibly over because of a tragic decision. He calls me collect once a month. He is really sorry for what he did. He understands the punishment, respects it, and doesn't question it. He attends AA meetings while serving time.

It should be obvious why Henry touches me so deeply. I am in recovery. I could have done something as tragic as what Henry did. I shudder at the idea of it. But the important thing is that Henry is in recovery, too. He can't undo what happened. All he can do is try to go forward. Henry is doing that. He is being accountable. I am proud of him.

SIX

BE WHERE YOUR FEET ARE

"Win the day" goes back to Bear Bryant. He used to say to his players every single day, "I just want you to get just a little bit better." Nick Saban focused on being better than yesterday. Kirby Smart told his players, "Outwork yesterday." I've employed all of those versions at some point. The one that I think provides the best solution came from Kevin Elko, whom Coach Saban regularly brought in to speak to Alabama players. He phrased it as "Be where your feet are." Focus on one play at a time. Focus on one moment at a time.

Being where your feet are is a great way to quiet your mind. If you look too far ahead, that's where you find your anxiety. If you look to the past, that's where you find your regret. That's why I encourage my players to stay right in the present. That's where they can concentrate just on getting better.

Like most of the concepts in this book, being where your feet are is easier to understand than it is to execute. College athletes have so much they want to accomplish, most of it, give or take a day, by tomorrow. I remind them that becoming the best player they can be is the ultimate eating of the elephant. The beauty of this approach is that it takes a lot of stress off their shoulders. Players at top programs are saddled with high expectations, the hype of being highly recruited, the hope of their family and friends. If I can convince them to be where their feet are, to perform the task in front of them, it takes away the stress of "I've got to do this. I've got to do that. Everyone is counting on me."

That's outside noise, as Coach Saban called it. The public understands the distractions that afflict the stars they know. There's publicity and celebrity and all that those issues entail. There's the lure of the NFL and, inherent in that, the rush to mature. Now there's the added responsibilities that come with the amount of money going to the top players. But the freshmen who come in have distractions that are just as difficult, if not more so, to handle. Everyone understands the adjustments that come with entering college: leaving home, harder academics, the responsibility that comes with independence. Add to that all that a freshman football player must handle: physical training that's way more demanding than anything he did in high school; integrating himself into a locker room filled with older, more physically and mentally mature players; learning how to handle the sudden arrival of money in his pocket, courtesy of name, image, and likeness income; and the toughest thing of all: not receiving the instant gratification that comes from playing. You, the freshman player, begin to train with me. You're bigger, faster, stronger, and better than you've ever been. But you're not on the field. You've never watched from the sideline. From the time you started playing, there was a team for you: middle school, freshman, junior varsity. You've never watched. And now you're an eighteen-year-old competing with twenty- to twenty-two-year-old teammates who have been working at this level of preparation for a lot longer than you have.

That realization would hit the freshmen every year like clockwork in the first two weeks of the season. They had been in school long enough that it was getting hard. Mom and Dad at home were asking, "Why aren't you playing? You're better than that guy" (that guy at Alabama usually on his way to being a high NFL draft pick). I tried to explain to the freshmen that the guy in front of them went through this same frustration two or three years ago.

When parents started trying to advocate for their kid, I tried to get in front of it. Who else is going to curtail it? I always tried to be the truth-teller to the players, so why not to the parents? They need to understand that the kid is calling because he has no one else to complain to, not because they need the parent to fix it. They need Mom's shoulder to cry on. I had that conversation many times. I'd tell them, "It's awesome that you have that good a relationship with your kid, but that's why he's coming to you, not because he needs you to change something."

Freshmen carry so many expectations and hopes, theirs and others. They are high-achieving kids who haven't failed very often, and now all of a sudden, they're up against something. They're at a level they've never been before. If I can convince them to be where their feet are, they no longer have to answer *How am I going to get on the field?*

Instead, I want them to think, *How about I just run the sprint with everything I have?*

That's not as simple as it sounds. Focusing only on the task at hand is not sexy. A lot of times it's not even fun. It's redundant. It's boring. It's running sprints in hundred-degree heat in the summer, pushing yourself to the point where you lose your lunch, and then pushing yourself some more. I don't like to think of it as redundancy. I think of it as consistency. The players depended on me to bring the same energy every day. Freddie Roach remembered thinking about me, "He made sure everyone was on the same page. He didn't have a bad day, and if he did, it wasn't known. You didn't understand it was a bad day."

Consistency means performing the task in front of you when you are expected to perform it. For instance, we had four or five lift groups scheduled over the course of the day. Take the 7 a.m. group. I wanted the players in the group lined up at the door of the weight room. At 6:59, I wanted every single player dressed identically: socks pulled up, shirt tucked in, wearing the same shoes as everyone else. You know, like a uniform. If you weren't on the line, dressed appropriately, at 7:00:00, then the entire group not only waited to cross into the room, but the entire group all performed the same penalty that you earned for not being ready. Being where your feet are includes accountability.

If the fear of punishment didn't work, what did I need to do to convince the players to do what I needed them to do?

I started by listening. I listened to their worst-case scenarios. I asked them to spell that out for me. *What is your fear? What are you so afraid of?* And they talked that out. I explained to them that they could manage that fear, and that they were worrying about something that they couldn't control. The worst wasn't even that bad. Jalen Hurts fumbled the first snap he took at Alabama. Tua Tagovailoa's first pass in college football? He threw an interception. Nobody talks about that.

In 2019, we had a sophomore running back named Jerome Ford. He started our opener against Duke because two backs ahead of him, Najee Harris and Brian Robinson, had been suspended for the first half. Early in the game, Jerome fumbled at our 26-yard line. That's pretty much where you could mark the end of the world for him. Jerome had to be the guy, and he fumbled.

He came back to the sideline, his head down. I went over and asked him, "You don't think Mark Ingram ever fumbled? Ingram fumbled, and you fumbled, and it's not about the fumble. Get your ass back out there and carry the ball. Do what you do."

Ford ran for a 37-yard touchdown and led us in rushing that day.

Quinnen Williams is a good example. Quinnen had been playing the edge, what we used to call a defensive end, for two years, one year on the scout team, one year as a backup. Before spring practice 2018, Coach Saban told Quinnen he wanted him to move to nose guard, the interior of the line, a job often described as playing in a closet. Quinnen came into my office, and he was freaking out. Our nose guards all had been big men, plugging up the middle, guys like Terrence Cody and Jesse Williams. The depth chart said that Quinnen weighed 285, which might have been right if he wore all his equipment and filled his pockets with change.

"You want me to play that position now, and I only weigh 275 pounds," Quinnen said. "This is my year. This is my chance. How am I gonna ever get on the field? If he's got me playing nose, I'm not big enough."

He had anxiety oozing from every pore, trying to figure out how to handle a new position and prove himself on a team that demanded excellence. I brought him back to where his feet were.

"Instead of focusing on 'I'm supposed to do this,' 'I'm supposed to do that,'" I said, "how about you just work on getting your hands stronger?"

He worked on that one step instead of thinking about his comfort zone being on the outside, where he could rush the passer. By the sixth practice of spring ball, Quinnen came into my office dancing. "They can't block me. I may weigh 275, but they can't block me. You'll get me to 300, right?"

"Yeah, I'll get you there," I said.

"They can't block me. This is the best thing I've ever done."

He made All-American that year. The next spring, the Jets made him the third pick in the NFL draft. Quinnen has been an All-Pro defensive tackle and gone to the last three Pro Bowls.

Ryan Kelly is another good example. We repeated as national champion his second season. We were back at the White House, and he was looking around. He said, "That's what I want to do."

"What?" I said.

"I want to be in the Secret Service," he said.

I burst out laughing.

"What's so funny?" he asked.

"Look," I said, "I will introduce you to whomever you need to know to get you that job one day, but you're going to play in the NFL."

"Cochran, I'm not going to play in the NFL," he said. "I haven't touched the field! There's no way I'm playing in the NFL."

"Do you have three years of eligibility left? You're about to be the guy."

He started to explain how he wasn't at the top of the depth chart. I told him to forget about that. Work hard and work on technique. Beat the man across the line of scrimmage. Don't worry about who else is snapping the ball between their legs. Ryan won the starting job for the 2013 season. By 2015, his redshirt senior season, he became an All-American. Indianapolis drafted him in the first round, which he turned down to join the Secret Service.

Just kidding. Ryan has played in four Pro Bowls, and after nine seasons with the Colts, he's now a Minnesota Viking.

SKULL SESSION

I get it. All of us worry about worst-case scenarios. The night before my first Fourth Quarter workout in my new job at West Alabama, I didn't sleep. I lay there in bed, worrying that I would yell like I always did in Fourth Quarter workouts and the yelling would trigger another migraine, the kind of migraines that I turned to prescription painkillers to relieve. How would I handle it?

I used a megaphone, I didn't yell so much, and I didn't get another migraine.

I always liked the saying "See a little, see a lot. See a lot, see nothing." That's a corollary of being where your feet are. I tell my players that they shouldn't worry about the worst-case scenario, but they should prepare for it. Worrying about things you can't control is a waste of energy. If there are steps you can take to assert control over your doubts and fears, you owe it to yourself to take those steps. There's no scenario where anxiety is helpful. You have to control the controllables.

One other thing: Performing the task in front of you doesn't mean that you are ignoring or delaying the overall goal. Sometimes, you can do both at once. It's kind of like in the fourth quarter of a game, and you hear a fan pleading, "We need a touchdown!" Actually, what the quarterback needs to do is execute the next play. If he does that, you never know. At LSU, in 2012, our chance of winning a second straight national championship didn't look good. We trailed the No. 5 Tigers, 17–14, with the ball on our 28-yard line and 1:27 to play. They could probably hear the Tiger Stadium crowd in New Orleans. AJ McCarron had completed one of seven passes in the second half for zero yards. AJ didn't try to make up for the failure of the passing game all at once. In the next five plays, he completed four passes. On the last one, from the LSU 28 yard line, AJ threw a short screen pass to T.J. Yeldon. AJ didn't take the snap saying "We're gonna score a touchdown right here." He took the snap saying "I'm gonna throw a good ball." T.J. caught it, broke a tackle, juked his way to the sideline, and sprinted into the end zone. We won the game, 21–17. We went on to win our second straight BCS title.

AJ went to the sideline, sat down on the bench, and just sobbed. I guess the tension released and the excitement of making a big play at a critical time overwhelmed him. That's the epitome of being right there in the moment.

SKULL SESSION

That moment sticks with me because I'm not a crier. I look at crying, and I can't do it. I told my dad, "When you pass away, I'll do the eulogy, because I don't think I can cry." And yet, in rehab, I cried like a baby. I think in rehab, the combination of the sleep deprivation, the physical toll of withdrawal, and all my fears overrode my defenses. I had so many fears: that I would lose my job, that I wouldn't be adequate without the pills, that people are going to always look at me as an addict and never again as a coach, that I would never be taken seriously or be trusted.

After a while, you figure out that all those worries about things that might happen are not as bad as the disease you are trying to conquer. For a long time, it conquered me.

SEVEN

ADDICTION

The first migraines I remember getting hit me on game days when I worked with the high school kids at LSU. I got them from yelling. But I didn't yell that much, and once I popped a couple of Advils, the headaches went away. You know, like normal people. At the Hornets, I hardly yelled at all. I was an assistant, there weren't that many players, and they were professional athletes. I would say they were grown men and not kids, but that wasn't always the case. Anyway, I think it's fair to say that I found my voice when I left the NBA for Tuscaloosa.

It is a loud voice.

I yelled a lot. I am loud. I yelled to get their attention. I yelled to let them know that we came to work. I tried not to yell to scold them. I yelled to juice up my players, to generate enthusiasm for everything I wanted them to accomplish in this workout, on that station, during this one rep. I yelled to be Coach Yeah!Yeah!Yeah!Yeah!Yeah! If I got juiced up, they did better. They coached each other better, and then I didn't have to scream as much, because yelling is where my headaches really came from, especially in the heat of an Alabama summer.

I remember one time I closed my eyes and took deep breaths because my head hurt so much I was seeing spots. One of the players said, "You taking a nap, Coach?"

I thought, *God, if you only knew how much pain I'm in right now.* But I couldn't show it. I couldn't falter in front of those guys when I preached to them that they couldn't falter.

Mary Ray-Allen is the wife of Jeff Allen, the longtime trainer at Alabama and one of my closest friends. Mary is a speech pathologist on the university faculty. When I was groping for a solution to my migraines, along about 2010, I went to her office, and they put cameras on me. They filmed me yelling, because I never lost my voice. And it didn't make sense, because every coach would lose his voice during preseason camp. Their film study showed that when I yell, I use my calves, my hamstrings, my glutes, my back, my traps; all of my muscles contracted.

Maybe that's why I didn't lose my voice. And maybe that also had a hand in the pain I experienced. All that energy would flow from my body into my head, which didn't have room for it.

Mary and her colleagues suggested some changes to how I yelled, but I couldn't do what they asked. I had doctors suggest "Stop yelling." They may as well have said "Stop working." Someone suggested that I use a microphone. Amplify my voice? Need help to do my job? No, sir. I believed that Coach Saban and the players would think I had gotten soft. I wouldn't even wear a mic when I spoke at banquets before hundreds of people. That amount of talking at that decibel level would exhaust me.

I was too macho to admit that I needed help, even for something as trivial as amplifying my voice. That attitude would come back to haunt me.

SKULL SESSION

By 2012, the migraines settled in for what seemed to be a long-term lease. Cissy thought the migraines came from stress, and when I didn't talk about them at home anymore, she figured I had solved the problem. Which I had. It was the way that I solved the problem that became the bigger problem, the problem that eventually threatened my life.

I had gone through a number of solutions, prescribed and otherwise. I tried blood thinners. I tried beta blockers, which keep adrenaline from going to work on blood vessels. Neither worked. I tried breathing pure oxygen. I tried dunking my head in a bucket of ice, which helped but, let's face it, is not a long-term solution. Neither was massaging Tiger Balm salve into my temples to increase the blood flow where the migraines felt the worst. That would help for a few minutes. I will confess to using Icy Hot cream on my body to kick-start my energy for a workout, but that's different from trying to stop a migraine.

Enter opioids. My doctor brought up the option of Vicodin, which is a mixture of hydrocodone and acetaminophen—you know, Tylenol. Vicodin is the drug that sank its teeth into Brett Favre, the long-time NFL quarterback. My doctor warned me that

ADDICTION

Vicodin could be addictive. I waved him off. Addicted? Me? Get outta here! I am the strength coach at the University of Alabama. I make a lot of money. I don't show weakness. There's no way I will ever become dependent on anything but hard work and enthusiasm.

I didn't exactly show a real grasp of how addiction works.

Vicodin didn't work for me either, so then we moved to extended-release oxycodone. Bingo! Hallelujah! Talk about a miracle drug! I could coach all day and not have a hangover or a headache the next morning. Problem solved. Except that it stopped working unless I used more, and I kept using more, and by the time I realized I had a problem, it was because I ran out of pills and became sick as a dog.

That was 2015, three years after my first prescription. I was snorting ten pills a day. I have a history of alcoholism in my family; that's why my parents rarely drank. But it never occurred to me that addiction would be an issue. None of that registered. Hey, I survived growing up in New Orleans, a partying town.

Kirby Smart and I first started working together at LSU. We became close friends on Coach Saban's staff. Kirby left Alabama to become head coach at Georgia after we won the 2015 national championship. A year later, another close friend, Lane Kiffin, who had been on the Alabama staff for three seasons, left Tuscaloosa. He had agreed to become the head coach at Florida Atlantic University after our season ended. But Coach Saban fired Lane on a Sunday morning shortly after the offense sputtered in a playoff semifinal win over Washington.

Maybe it was coincidence, maybe not. All I know is that once Kirby and Lane left, my addiction got awful. Kirby had been Coach's right-hand guy and had been with him going back to LSU. I took over that role. Coach Saban really leaned on me. When Kirby left, it fell to me to be the guy people came to in order to test drive what they wanted to say to Coach Saban. They thought I knew everything because I had survived for so long.

Did that additional responsibility contribute to my issues? I honestly don't know. What I do know is I couldn't stop taking pills. *Could. Not. Stop.* And nobody had a clue.

I should make one quick point: I am not an alcoholic. I have never been addicted to alcohol. I haven't taken a drink since my first trip to rehab in

ADDICTION

2020. My point is that I've never had blackouts. I don't have periods of time during my addiction that I don't remember. Good and bad, I remember it all.

One reason I could hide my addiction is that my work environment allowed me to isolate myself from everyone. I had the weight room away from all the other coaches. I had my own turf. We built a big, beautiful new training facility in 2019, the one that became famous for the decorative waterfall. I had twenty-five thousand square feet filled with weight stations, a smoothie bar, and all manner of bells, not to mention whistles. Upstairs, we had half again that space, filled with cardio equipment and some offices, including a locker room for the former Alabama players now in the NFL. In that locker room there was a little meeting room. I could go up there and lock that door, and I couldn't have been more hidden away. I'd take out my pills, crush them on the table with a credit card, snort them, wipe off the table, and go back to work. To answer your next question, I snorted them because I quickly got to the point in my addiction where taking them orally didn't work.

Anyway, that room came in handy because I had reached the point where I couldn't last three hours without more pills. I could get in there and get out without anyone missing me. Game days got a little trickier. No—game days got a *lot* trickier.

The only way I could get the privacy I needed was to be in the locker room practically by myself. As a strength coach, I could hang back, do what I needed to do, and come out for pregame warm-ups a little bit late. Or I could come in off the field a little bit early, pretending as if I were doing something for a player. The only door in the locker room that locked was the head coach's office. We had a number of female trainers and nutritionists in the locker room. When the team went out onto the field, that would be their chance to use the bathroom. I figured if I went into Coach Saban's locker room, it would look like I did so out of courtesy. So I would go in there and lock the door. Coach had a counter in his bathroom that I could use to crush the pills.

When I got to Georgia, I wasn't the strength coach any longer, so I had a little different pregame schedule. I coordinated the special teams, so I had to be on the field while they did their work. But special teams warmed up early, finishing before the rest of the team. I would go back into the locker room and go to Kirby's office and pretend as if I were using his bathroom.

ADDICTION

Halftimes were harder to figure out, especially for road games. I'd have to use a stall, and that was not easy, because there's a limited amount of time and a lot of people who need the bathroom. A coaches' locker room might have two stalls, and at some stadiums, you don't even have a door on the stall (some schools take pride in how spartan the accommodations for visiting teams are). But I did what I needed to do, and I never once walked out of the bathroom with residue around my nose. How did that not happen? I usually had no mirrors and less time. Once or twice, I would put my phone in selfie mode and check my nose. But whatever I did I had to be fast.

The last game I coached at Alabama, we played Michigan in the Capital One Bowl in Orlando on New Year's Day 2020. I went into the coaches' locker room at halftime and used a stall because there was no office. I snorted my pills off the little plastic shelf above the toilet paper dispenser. The next day, Ellis Ponder, our football operations guy and a longtime assistant to Coach Saban, asked me, "Did you snort something in the stall? Someone heard a sound like you were snorting something."

I just looked at him and said, "What are you talking about?" And that's as far as it went.

Look, there's so much pressure trying to maintain Alabama's success, everyone worries about their own issues. They didn't pay a whole lot of attention to me. And if they did, they still weren't experts in addiction. That's the thing with pills: You can't tell unless you know what to look for, and you have to actually look for it. Guys who smoke weed or do cocaine leave a lot more clues. The main physical tell with the pills I took is that your pupils become "pinned," as in the size of pinpricks. No one even thought to look, because no one expected a thing. Well, almost no one.

Linda Leoni, Coach's longtime administrative assistant, said to me one time during the season, "Man, you've had a cold for a while."

"It's just this doggone pollen," I said.

I'm no plant expert, but I've lived in the South my whole life, and I know that pollen shows up in the spring, not the fall. But Linda never said another word. I have never blamed Linda for not noticing. People either don't suspect the worst, or don't want to suspect the worst.

ADDICTION

In the moment, I thought I was pretty slick. I thought I hid everything, kept all the balls I juggled in the air to keep my life going. By the time I got to 2019, which would be my last year at Alabama, the three people I was closest to thought something was amiss.

Cissy and I had begun to drift apart. In and of itself, that's not all that unusual for couples who have been married twenty years. I had a high-pressure job, and Cissy managed the house and three young children. That can put anyone, husband or wife, on the Olympic teeth-grinding team. When you throw a pill addiction into that mix... well, it's a miracle that Cissy stayed with me. Being a coach's wife is, by definition, solitary. Being a strength coach's wife, when the strength coach spends more time with the players than anyone on the staff, takes a woman with inordinate patience, a willingness to have football players wandering in and out of the house at all times, and a willingness to do a lot of parenting on her own.

On top of all that, she married an addict. I grew increasingly irritable, and while I kept the balls in the air as best I could at the office, at home I

SKULL SESSION

dropped one or two. That's how it always is, right? We take our frustrations out on the ones we love. Cissy and I fought a lot. We had a lot of tension, a lot of living parallel lives. Looking back, it was a miserable existence. She thought I didn't love her. I think it got really bad when I drank. If I had the next day off, I'd have a couple of drinks that night, and we would fight like cats and dogs.

To celebrate both of us turning forty in 2019, we decided to take a Mediterranean cruise. You would think after our honeymoon cruise into Hurricane Katrina that we would steer clear of ships, but no. It took a year's worth of planning for us to leave for two and a half weeks. Cissy and I were both anxious about leaving for that amount of time. Beau, Savannah, and Lucy stayed with Cissy's parents. Cissy says now she knew I wasn't 100 percent, but she didn't know why.

We got over to Europe and boarded the ship, and it made a couple of stops in Greece, a couple in Italy, and along about day 10, we went to Rome, which is where I ran out of pills. We had about a week to go, and I had no pills. My body didn't care that I was on vacation with my wife, my only vacation of the year, and that I was in one of the great

ADDICTION

cities of Europe. I started to go through withdrawal. I started sweating like I was back home running two-a-days, the flulike symptoms attacked, and I had to hang on as best I could. Cissy asked me what was wrong, and I told her I was struggling because I had run out of dip. Copenhagen is not a big seller in Rome. She believed me, because why wouldn't she?

Copenhagen might have helped, but without that, and without pills, I turned to vodka, a good amount of vodka, which got me through the rest of the trip and the flight home. Two cruises, two bad experiences.

Not too long ago, to tease her, I suggested we take another cruise.

"Hell, no!" she said. "That was the last one."

We kept talking, and then she looked at me and said, "There's a lot of times that you know you shouldn't be here because of what you've done. It's unbelievable. It's a miracle. Somebody's watching over you and has a better plan for you than you even know, because you did about everything you could to check out."

She's not wrong.

Cissy didn't see the addiction, but Cissy is a civilian. After we got home, as the 2019 season got underway, the two health professionals I worked with the most, two people I grew really close with, thought something was amiss.

Ginger Gilmore served as the assistant athletic director of behavioral health and wellness at Alabama. She helped a lot of athletes stay mentally healthy. Coach hired her because he believed that the young men on his team might tell a woman things that they wouldn't tell a male coach. As always, pretty shrewd thinking on his part. Ginger is a pro. We talked through ways to motivate individuals as well as the entire team. Once a month or so I would go into her office and close the door and even talk to her myself.

Jeff Allen remains the head athletic trainer at Alabama. Jeff is the best at what he does, and we worked hand in glove to make sure the players could perform at their best. That's what a strength coach and a trainer should do, but that isn't always the case. Their egos get in the way. The strength coach thinks the trainer is babying the player, or the trainer thinks the strength coach is ignoring the player's well-being. Jeff and I trusted each other professionally. We spoke as one voice—although he doesn't yell—and the players understood that the

ADDICTION

training room was an extension of my conditioning work. Jeff told them they couldn't come in there to hide, that his job was the same as mine.

Both Ginger and Jeff had suspicions about me that last year at Alabama.

Ginger saw how jumpy I had become. She knew I had a prescription for Adderall, but she wondered how much I was doing. She used the word "fluctuate." She saw my personality fluctuate. She saw my weight fluctuate. Man, at the height of my addiction I lost about thirty-five pounds. I called a doctor to get me on testosterone to keep up my weight. I went from 215 pounds to about 180, and the thing was, I was trim. Ripped to shreds. "You must work out all the time," someone said to me. I wasn't working out much at all. I got told daily, "Damn, you look good!" That's not exactly an incentive to stop using.

Ginger thought it was all because of the stress of my job. She described me as being on autopilot at a pace that no one could sustain. She worried about the toll it continued to take on me. She kept her door open to me, and I would come into her office and unload. I'd tell her how I felt like I had to fix everything, how I felt like I was letting this person or that person down. I needed affirmation that I was doing the right thing, that I was making a difference. She would tell me I couldn't do everything, and I would nod, and say no, I can't do everything, and then I would walk out of her office and resume trying to do everything and fix everyone.

Sometimes at team meetings Ginger would discuss something with the players, a mental wellness program she intended to conduct, and I would come in behind her when she finished and say, "No, we're doing heavy squats today." She would get mad, but I could get away with it because that was my personality—bravado, pride, and arrogance. They didn't always serve me so well, but Ginger stuck with me and remains a good friend.

Jeff saw the arrogance, too. Jeff is earnest. He is a spiritual man who doesn't flaunt his religion. Jeff is just a good person. And he probably feels worse about not picking up on what I went through than anyone.

"Your role was so much more than a strength coach, and it really took a toll," Jeff said. "Trying to take care of everybody, you probably didn't take care of yourself like you should have. Being a passionate guy who cared and cared about winning and cared about the kids, and poured your heart into them, I think that had a lot to do with what you went through. The way that you coached is physically exhausting. I've never seen somebody coach like that. And I think it really, really took a toll. I think it wore you out literally, physically and emotionally, trying to be everything, to everybody, but it was from a good place. It was from a genuine place."

In the moment, in 2019, Jeff knew something had gone awry, but he couldn't put his finger on what. You know how with a close work colleague, your relationship approaches something like a marriage? There are a lot of mental shortcuts. You can finish each other's sentences. Jeff felt like I had become disconnected, that I wasn't as engaged as I had been. He said I remained steady enough to look like I was getting everything done, but he landed on the word *erratic*. If that doesn't describe an addict, nothing does.

I thought I had covered all my tracks. But the numbers don't lie, and the fact is, our players didn't make gains in the weight room that season like they usually did. When that happened in the past, we would put our heads together and talk about it, pick each other's brains. What do we need to do? If we had a string of injuries, what do we need to change? Are we working the players too hard? Jeff and I would plot our strategy, then go to Coach Saban and make our case: We're doing too much. We need to cut back. Let's try this, or that.

Jeff says he tried to bring my behavior up to me quite a few times, and that as he tried to confront me, I began to distance myself from him. I can say now that our relationship began to strain.

Which makes this a good time to discuss how my confidence had begun to overflow into arrogance. That last year is when Regions Bank asked me to appear in a commercial. You have to understand that Coach Saban didn't allow his assistants to have a public profile. He spoke for the program. Yet, as time went on, he loosened that rule for me. In 2013, when Armen Keteyian did a *60 Minutes* piece on Alabama football, Coach allowed Armen to do a separate feature on me.

And, of course, there was the Coach Yeah video of me imploring the fans in Bryant-Denny to make some noise that played right before kickoff. I have to admit that made me even more like a celebrity. I made sure that the other assistants knew I didn't

ADDICTION

think I was any better than they are, but there's no question that my head had swelled. By 2019, there were times when I was pretty sure I was the reason that Alabama football stood atop the college football world, and I actually let Jeff know it. I pray to God that those sentiments were the pills talking, warping my reality. My ego was certainly warped.

After I told Jeff about my addiction, he felt a lot of guilt, as if he of all people should have picked up on it. "I regret never coming right out and saying, 'Hey, man, are you taking something?'" Jeff said. "It's been a lesson for me. Because sometimes it crosses my mind. If something would have happened, it would have broken me, because deep down in my heart, I knew it."

Jeff feels bad because he hesitated, and one of the reasons he hesitated is the stigma of addiction.

"I didn't confront it like I should have," he said. "We didn't want to know it. Part of me was like, 'What are we going to do? We're going to send Scott Cochran to rehab? What kind of image will this create for the Alabama football program? What kind of image does this project for Coach Saban?' I should have put all that stuff aside to help my friend. And I didn't do it. Part of me is like, 'Did I give up on him? Did I just kick him to Athens instead of trying to save him here?'"

I told you he was a good person.

When Jeff tried to apologize to me, I stopped him midsentence. "Dude," I said, "this is nothing you could have stopped. There's no way." And I can't argue with him thinking about what was best for Alabama football. We all had that job. He just performed it better than I did.

When the 2019 season ended, and I went to Jeff and told him I was thinking about going to Georgia to work for Kirby, he didn't try to talk me out of it. Of course, he didn't understand that I was leaving to try to outrun my addiction. He just thought I needed a change, and that both Alabama and I would benefit.

One thing he and I agree on is that I needed to leave in order to save my life. Jeff thinks if I had stayed at Alabama, the addiction would have surfaced and I might have been more resistant to getting help. I don't know if that's the case, but he's right about one thing. I had to take the Georgia job to realize that the addiction came with me. My plan to leave it in the weight room at Alabama failed.

ADDICTION

Trying to outrun my addiction was the main reason I wanted to leave. I had others. I wanted to make a million dollars. I wanted to be a head coach, which would have achieved the million-dollar goal. It didn't bother me that strength coaches don't become head coaches. If I'm honest, my pursuit of a head coaching job had everything to do with my ego. I wanted to be a head coach because I wanted the money and the power. Here's where my thinking was:

I thought, *I can do what Coach Saban does.*

I thought, *Kirby's my best friend. He's a knucklehead. I can do that.*

Delusional, anyone?

As you may imagine, Coach Saban didn't take my departure well. I had been his guy. He trusted me. He listened to me. But he felt like he paid me well and I should be happy. He understood how close Kirby and I had been. But Kirby had tried to get me to leave with him four years earlier, and I hadn't. Coach Saban thought that ship had sailed. He had no idea what I was going through.

Once I told him I intended to leave, what Coach Saban saw is that I intended to leave to go work for Alabama's rival for SEC and national supremacy.

He held me to the buyout clause in my contract. To go to another SEC school, the contract said I owed 33 percent of what remained. I had three years left, so I owed Alabama a year's salary: $600,000. The lawyers negotiated and eventually got it down to about half that, but that was still six figures per year over the next few years coming out of my pocket. I took a pay cut to go to Georgia, and I had to pay the first installment of my buyout. I didn't blink. That's how much I felt like I needed to leave.

EIGHT

THE ROAD TO RECOVERY

So you know what happened my first spring at Georgia: I nearly died. At the time nobody outside of me, Cissy, our families, and my medical people knew it. My medical people included Chris Herren, the former NBA player whose professional career got waylaid by addiction. He has been substance-free since 2008 and now is a motivational speaker and the operator of a rehab center in Massachusetts, right near the Rhode Island state line. We had him come speak to the Alabama team for several years. Chris delivers a riveting message, one that our players heard but I certainly never did.

On that fateful Easter weekend in 2020, Cissy remembered Chris's name, looked up his number in my phone, and called him Saturday.

"You don't know who I am, but you know Scott," Cissy said. She told him what she found and she told him what happened.

"He definitely needs help," Chris said. "I've got a place for him. Tell him to come up here."

The next day, Easter Sunday, I called Chris and began to turn what had been a business friendship into a much more meaningful relationship. On Monday, Cissy and I got on a flight to New England. Because this happened during the COVID pandemic, travel protocols had become strict. When we landed, Cissy didn't even leave the terminal. I walked out to baggage claim to meet Chris's people, and she turned around and got back on a plane to go home.

The fentanyl may have nearly killed me literally but the withdrawal from the opiates...well, there can't be anything worse. There is such a thing as MAT protocol—medication-assisted treatment—but Herren Wellness doesn't use MAT for opiates. "You're gonna want to kill yourself," they told me. "But you're not going to die from it."

Gee, thanks.

You feel like you have the worst kind of flu. Whatever I had inside me came out of both ends, and I couldn't sleep. My Fitbit logged eight hours of sleep for the first eight days. Not to mention that, since no one at Georgia knew I had gone to rehab, I continued to log in for staff meetings and recruiting calls. I remember calling offensive tackle Amarius Sims in, of all places, Cochran, Ga.

"Where you at, Coach?"

"Oh, I'm at my brother's lake house in Mississippi. The Wi-Fi isn't very good here."

Actually, I was in Seekonk, Massachusetts, but in a cabin that, if you didn't look too closely, might pass for a lake house in Mississippi.

I was in hell—no sleep for five nights straight, no medicine, just suffering. In desperation, I tried praying, but my mind was so jumpy it was hard to complete a thought.

I grew up Catholic, went to church every Sunday, and attended Catholic school. Faith was a big part of my upbringing, but I'd grown immune to it. That changed during my first round of withdrawals. The first couple of nights, I was saying my Hail Marys, my Our Fathers, and didn't feel like anything happened. On the third night I started to actually connect, talk to God, ask Him to guide me through the crazy and help me stay sober in the future. I told Him I couldn't take it anymore. He gave me thirty minutes of sleep. The next night, I did the same thing, and I got an hour of sleep. By the fifth night, the sixth night, he gave me two hours. I guess you'd say faith hit me. That little sliver of peace felt like a miracle. It was like God saying, "I've got you."

I stayed at Herren Wellness less than a month. Cissy and I were so naïve. Oh, you go to rehab for thirty days or so, you come back, and you're "fixed." I got detoxed and went back home, and a couple of weeks later, we moved to Athens. What could go wrong?

That first year at Georgia would have been a big adjustment even if I hadn't been in recovery. I had new responsibilities in a new place. Kirby hired me to coach the special teams and to implement and lead the team's Skull Sessions. I wasn't there two months before my new sobriety crumbled in the face of my ambition. I started taking pills again, crushing and snorting them. In Athens, as in Tuscaloosa, I kept my addiction to myself.

THE ROAD TO RECOVERY

We hadn't gotten very deep into the 2020 season before I understood that this Georgia team, as talented as it was, didn't have the right mindset to be a champion. Our players still kept one eye on the scoreboard. We were at least a year away, which was just as well, because the Alabama team I left behind won twelve of its thirteen games by at least two touchdowns, including a 41–24 defeat of the Georgia Bulldogs at Bryant-Denny Stadium in October. The way we lost that one told the difference between the two teams. We led 24–20 at the half. Alabama shut us out in the second half. We had two snaps in the red zone after halftime. Bama dominated us.

That was a weird day. I was on the opposite sideline of where I had been for thirteen years. Cissy and the kids had seats on the "wrong" side of the stadium, tucked in the corner of the end zone. She walked into Bryant-Denny with every nerve on high alert. Was I okay? Was I not okay? The last six months had shown her how little she knew about her husband. Would being back at Bryant-Denny trigger something emotionally for me? She told me later that she felt like she was on the verge of throwing up every waking second.

SKULL SESSION

The game did trigger something emotional. After it ended, I stayed on the field for a half hour, surrounded by my former Alabama players, whom I loved and who, I found out, still loved me. It didn't make the loss feel any better, but those players sure made me feel better.

We finished 8–2 that season, with a last-second defeat of undefeated Cincinnati in the Chick-fil-A Peach Bowl that I'll get to later in the book, and I was in the same boat I had been a year earlier: using again, trying to keep all the balls in the air without anyone discovering my secret. By the spring of 2021, I was taking more pills than I had ever taken. In late June I told Cissy I wanted to go back to Herren Wellness for a "refresher"; you know, go through the hell of detox, get a couple of weeks of counseling, turn around, and get back to Athens before anyone realized I had left.

When I checked in, they gave me a drug test. When the results came back, they showed no Adderall, no oxycodone. All they showed was fentanyl. They told me, "You're going to die. If this is what you're using, you're going to die."

They explained to me that on this stay, I needed to undergo the treatment that I didn't get on my first visit, that this would be a lengthy stay. Right about then, Cissy was coming to Seekonk to spend time with me. She had never been to the facility; now she could get a sense of what I was doing, meet the therapists, and so on.

When we sat down, Chris Herren laid it out straight to Cissy.

"Hey, he's sick," Chris said. "This is not okay. He's a sick man. This is a disease. He needs real treatment. He can't just come for a short stay like he did last time. He needs to really buckle down. The therapists are recommending eight months. But I think six months will be fine."

Six months meant no football season. It meant I no longer could hide my addiction. If I thought at all about not going through the long-term treatment, Cissy set me straight.

"You're gonna have to stay here and get long-term help," she said, "and if you choose to come back to Athens instead, you can't live with us. You can go find yourself an apartment. I hope you choose to stay."

She said later it was the hardest thing she ever had to say. It was certainly hard to hear. I was terrified. I knew I had a huge problem. The treatment would be expensive, and I wouldn't be working. That was the other terrifying part. I would have to tell Kirby. This would be the second time I broke his heart. Almost six years earlier, when he left Alabama for Georgia, I shook his hand and told him I would come with him. But Coach Saban made me such an incredible offer to stay that I had to call Kirby and tell him I couldn't do it.

Now I had to call him and tell him I had to leave.

That night, I began to meditate, a coping skill that I learned at Herren Wellness. This complete calm washed over me. I heard God whisper, "Trust me." I heard Him say, "I got you. I got you. I carried you this far. I'm not gonna stop carrying you now." I thought about the coaching staff. Kirby had just hired Will Muschamp, his college teammate and a two-time head coach in the SEC. Will loves special teams. He'd probably gladly take them over. I'm not leaving the team in a bad place.

So I called Kirby the next morning, with Cissy sitting right next to me for support.

"You hired a drug addict," I said.

"What are you talking about?" Kirby replied.

I thought he was gonna fire me, yell at me, ask me how I could let him down like this. All Kirby said to me is "What can I do for you and your family?" I know Kirby said it, and I'll always love him for it, but I also think maybe God stepped in right there, too.

Kirby and I talked it through, and a few days later, Kirby and Drew Brannon, a colleague I had worked with in developing Skull Sessions for the Bulldogs, flew up to Massachusetts to see me. You have to understand how much that meant to me. A head coach like Kirby gets very little time off. He took one of his off days, drove ninety minutes to Atlanta, boarded a commercial flight to Boston, and drove ninety minutes to Seekonk, all for the chance to spend an hour with me. Then he turned around, drove back to the airport, and went home. A twelve-hour day, on his day off.

We sat and talked. It was right about then that the Southeastern Conference made the deal with Texas and Oklahoma to leave the Big 12 and come to the SEC in 2025 (it turns out they made a switch a year earlier than scheduled).

"Maybe you'll be out of here by then and help me coach some ball," Kirby said.

We all laughed; him tossing off that joke really put me at ease. *I don't need to rush*, I thought. *If I need to be here for six months, maybe I can do that.*

SKULL SESSION

Cissy always has been in charge of the money in our house. Addicts have to hide how they spend money. I remember telling her there was something I needed to buy for the weight room even though I had arranged for someone to donate it. I would take the money out of our checking account and buy pills with it.

When Cissy left Herren Wellness and went home, she swallowed hard and called Coach Saban. I had two years' worth of buyout payments to make, and now I had to pay for rehab, which is really expensive. Cissy told Coach that we wanted to honor the buyout. We would pay it. We didn't want to cause any problems, but we needed some extended time. Could he help us?

The next day, Coach called me and said, "Hey, you've paid enough of the buyout. Get healthy." That is him saying, "I love you. I care about you. Get better."

What a relief. That took a huge burden off my mind and allowed me to put that mental energy toward my rehab. One of the many ways in which I consider myself lucky is that I haven't fought rehab. I have sought treatment three times, and none of those times have I tried to cut corners. When the therapists broached the subject of me staying for several months, I didn't fight it. I trusted them. I wanted to get well.

I made sufficient progress that, after three months, the therapists granted me a weekend pass to fly home and see Cissy and our beautiful kids. Man, did I miss them. But I was doing so well that when I went back to Herren Wellness, I stayed for only another ten days or so before they released me. I stayed one hundred days, well short of the six months that the therapists predicted.

But the calendar said October, several weeks into the 2021 season, which Georgia and the rest of college football had started without me. I returned to Athens and offered to help Kirby in any manner that he saw fit. Kirby, like most of my closest friends, felt dumbstruck that he hadn't detected anything amiss and wanted to help me without knowing quite what to do. Not to mention that he was trying to coach a team to win the national championship.

The biggest way that Kirby helped me is that he didn't fire me. He didn't care about the possible stigma. He wanted me to get healthy, and he still believed that I could help the team. That sounds simple, but Kirby stuck out his neck for me. When I left, Kirby took me off the list of the ten assistant coaches who, according to NCAA rules, could coach the players on the field. The administration wanted him to cut my salary commensurate with my diminished duties.

He refused. He wanted me there to do what I have always done—connect to the players, listen to them, motivate them, just be there for them. When we won the national championship, pulling away from Alabama in the fourth quarter as our Alabama teams had done to so many opponents throughout my time there, no one would question Kirby's decisions. He stuck his neck out for me, which I never will forget.

It would be nice to say that upon my return to Athens, I maintained my good health and never looked at another dose of oxy again. It just wouldn't be accurate. Kirby put me back in charge of special teams for the 2022 season, when we went 15–0 and won a second consecutive national championship. I finally had gotten what I asked for, the chance to coach on the field, and the pressure I put on myself to perform, the hours that I devoted to making sure my coaching matched the performance that Kirby and

Georgia demanded, eventually made my personal defenses crumble. Because I was sober, I wasn't confident, and I couldn't handle going above and beyond all the time. I was so afraid to mess up special teams. I was trying to impress the kids and the coaches, and I had to put so much preparation into it. My nerves got out of whack, and I just got sick of it. I thought, *You know what? Forget this. I know how to fix this.*

So, as we got into the grind of the 2023 season, I started using again. I never descended to the hell I put myself in my last year at Alabama or my first eighteen months in Athens. I never took fentanyl again, which may be damning myself with faint praise, but at least I caught myself before I descended that far. I found a guy who had a prescription, so I knew the pills were real.

I started off at two pills a day, and then it became four. And then I would think, *Hey, I need two more for practice*, and I got up to six or eight pills a day.

At first, it felt as if once I started taking the pills, my meetings started going better. The pills propped up my ego. I was able to get out of my head and just work. It felt like the oxy helped me, like it was a super drug. The truth is that it put me back on the road to ruin. Getting the pills reintroduced me to the world of deception, to the never-ending problem of feeding the habit. I couldn't run out of oxy, because I would get sick again.

The worst experience I had came one afternoon as I planned my special teams meeting. I looked at the clock in my office. Okay, I've got fifty minutes. I can go meet a guy at the coffee shop and get two more pills so that I can get through practice. I hopped in my car, raced over there, got the pills, and then I was back in my car, looking at the dashboard clock, sitting in traffic, just watching the seconds tick off, thinking, "I'm gonna get caught. I'm gonna be late to practice. People are gonna find out." I couldn't park in my normal spot. At Georgia, my parking spot was right inside the gates at the football facility. So, I started thinking, if I was cutting the time too close, I would just park outside the gates and sneak in. I was already in my practice gear, and nobody would know.

These days, if I'm having a bad day, if I have the thought *Man, it would be a lot easier if I could use something again*, I think about that. I think about sitting in that traffic, watching the seconds tick off. I don't ever want to be in that hell again. Just thinking about it now kicks my ass. I don't ever want to be looking at that clock again on my dashboard. It gives me the worst feeling.

I don't have to feel that ever again.

We finished the regular season undefeated, the third straight year we did so, but lost the SEC Championship to Alabama and missed the playoff. We went to the Orange Bowl to play Florida State, a consolation prize for a team that expected to win championships.

But even that hollowness paled before the feeling of self-disgust I had in my gut. Once the chase for the big prize ended, it dawned on me.

Oh, shit.

No.

I thought I had this under control. I'm back where I don't want to be. I know what happens. I know how this story ends.

Cissy knew. She didn't know what she knew, but she knew. A couple of days before the game, the two of us were in our hotel room. She grabbed me and looked straight into my eyes.

"I know that you're struggling," Cissy said. "I don't know if you've used. I don't know if you haven't. I've seen some instances when your eyes are pinned. It could be my imagination."

Then she said the two sentences that saved my life again.

"But we no longer need to coach football after this season. This can be our last game."

Cue the violins. I'd love to tell you that I grabbed her and hugged her with tears in my eyes, relieved that she would love me if I never won another national championship. That emotion was in there. But that's not how I responded. Let's not forget that I had returned to active addiction. "Whatever," I said. "Shut up. What are you talking about, 'last game'? I'm not struggling. Look at me. I'm doing great. I'm going to AA meetings. I wish everybody would leave me alone."

Real life still isn't Hollywood.

But I did hear her. After we beat Florida State, I came home, and I was just done. I said to myself, *This is stupid. How did I get myself here again?* I was so disgusted with myself.

I told Kirby that I was struggling. This time around, he didn't blink. He told me that there's a good outpatient clinic near campus called the Commencement Center that people in the athletic department had used with good results. I drove over there and I called Cissy.

"I'm at the Commencement Center," I said. "Can you come over here?"

Ten minutes later, she walked in.

"You were right," I said. "I messed up."

"Give me the debit card. Now," she said.

Smart woman.

The nurse, who's also the psychologist, asked me, "So what do we do?"

"I don't know," I told her. "But I'm probably going to work on me." The outpatient program is a six-week commitment, and I resigned myself to the idea that it might last longer. But after about two weeks, I realized that I wouldn't be going back to Georgia.

"I can't do this anymore," I told Kirby. "I gotta take a break."

Honestly, at that moment, I thought that I would never coach again. I thought that maybe I would be a motivational speaker. Really, I didn't know what I would do.

The withdrawals this time weren't that bad, because I hadn't been taking as much. That was a good thing. They put me on Suboxone for two weeks to prevent withdrawals, and then they got me off that. Since the Commencement Center is an outpatient clinic, the disruption to my family life remained at a minimum.

My AA sponsor really helped me, too.

"It's definitely a relapse," he said, "but you had [been clean] before that happened. You had really good recovery time. Don't look at your relapse as being so bad. Look at it and say, okay, what happened?"

I realized I had stopped doing the work for recovery. I had so much else to do, trying to prove I could carry my weight as a special teams coach. I took recovery off my plate.

After I completed the six weeks, I began what the recovery process calls "mirroring." I volunteered at the Commencement Center every day from 8:30 a.m. to 1 p.m., running groups, helping people whose shoes I had been in a few weeks before. That bolstered my work in recovery, too, although it didn't spare me from emotional pain. Once I turned back to lend a hand to others, the first guy I sponsored died from an overdose. I had a really close friend in rehab whom I spoke to every Friday night before a game. He was a young guy, the age of the players I coached, a kid from New York who went to an elite boarding school. He overdosed and died. I've known a lot of people who died of an overdose. I am still here. How does that happen?

Knowing these people, good people, killed by this disease leaves me sad. But it also makes me pick up the phone when I get a direct message from someone who needs help.

I talk to people in every stage. The ones who tell you they have it figured out are the ones you worry about. They may listen, but they don't hear. The ones that call you and say, "Man, I'm struggling today," those are the people you can reach.

"Yes, you're asking me for help," I tell them. "You know you're struggling today. You know what? I'm struggling, too. I'm glad you called."

I became so enamored with the recovery work that I even considered buying the clinic.

Turns out that I am a football coach.

Recovery is another avenue of helping people, which, when you think about it, is what coaches do. I have talked about this with my friend and former colleague Steve Sarkisian, who as head coach has taken Texas to the last two College Football Playoff

SKULL SESSION

semifinals. Sark is in recovery, too, and we talk regularly, checking in on each other, giving each other support. Not long ago, we talked about wanting to help others the way that someone helped us. I said it always struck me as odd when you sit on an airplane and the flight attendant launches into the safety speech about putting your oxygen mask on first and then help your child. Your instinct is to do the opposite.

"That's kind of a snapshot of recovery, right?" Sark said. "You've got to take care of yourself first so that you can then take care of others."

Sark brought me to Austin to speak to his team before last season. He wanted them to hear the message that asking for help, showing vulnerability, is a sign of strength. Young men that age, Sark said, "are one of the most closed-off groups in our society, right? They hold things tight to the vest. They struggle at times with relationships. Being vulnerable for them is probably the one thing that takes the most courage. When you can display that courage, you start to become vulnerable. The courage to start to become vulnerable gives them a real sense of confidence that they can really go accomplish anything."

Sark loved that I could come in with my credentials and deliver that message. I'm thrilled that he thinks it helped.

The methods we employed at Alabama and Georgia to point our players in the right direction are effective outside the locker room, too. They remind me every day to do what's necessary to stay healthy as well as help develop my new team. You'll see how they easily they can be adapted for your goals, too.

NINE

LOVE, NOT FEAR

I became the head strength coach at the University of Alabama at the age of twenty-seven, and I was desperate to prove I could handle the job. On my drive into the office, I would tell myself that the weight room had flooded. Someone had broken a window. The whole place was a disaster. I had to be ready to fix it all and still get 105 players through a workout. I told myself all of those things and threw in a couple of dress-downs from Coach Saban, too. When I got to work and none of those catastrophes had happened—well, okay, Coach chewed me out more than once—I would just exhale and say, "Everything's gonna be great. We're gonna have a great day."

SKULL SESSION

I never thought I was good enough. I never played college football, so how could I be a good college strength coach? I established myself as the players' go-to coach. It was a natural fit, me being the strength coach. We spend more time with the players than anyone else on the staff. But let's face it. I was driven. I always told myself I had to overachieve, so I was going to find a way to plant more roots.

In other words, I motivated myself through fear, just like the two coaches who mentored me, Tommy Moffitt and Nick Saban. They believe in tough love. Moffitt invests a little more individually—as a strength coach, you have to—but he used fear like Coach Saban. Shoot, as I have described, Coach Saban could be intimidating to his assistants, let alone his players.

It's pretty obvious that fear works as a motivator. As I said, I used it on myself. When those catastrophes did happen, every five years or so, I was ready. But I paid a price in anxiety, in worry, in activating stress I didn't need. Lonny Rosen used to say, "You're wasting energy. You're already ready for the worst-case scenario. You're good at this. Don't worry about it."

LOVE, NOT FEAR

All of which is why I chose not to use fear to motivate players. I think love is the key. Love them through the hell because the work is gonna be hard, anyway. I feel like if you get to know somebody, you can push them when things get tough, because they know you have their back. When you can see the end result for them and tell them what's out there if they do the work, you can show them what they can become.

I think my methods stem from my parents: Mom worked so hard to help her students find jobs and careers; Dad used to write out a motivational quote and put it in my lunch every morning. In high school, all of my buddies at the lunch table would ask, "What's the quote?" Even when my lunch table included Moffitt and Vic Viloria, now the strength coach at Baylor, they liked the little jolt that comes from a motivational quote.

Now that I'm a head coach, I've got to make sure I hire at least one assistant who's a hardass. That's different from being mean. I hate coaches who take it out on the team if they're having a bad day. I can't stand those people. These kids are coming to work. They're coming to do everything they can to be great. You, the coach, have got to be at

SKULL SESSION

your best. You've got to set the tempo. There are times during the year when I'm no kindergarten teacher. There are certain things you can't negotiate on—the mental toughness, the running, the Fourth Quarter conditioning program, the weight room. It's hard. They don't want to be in there all the time. It's tough. There are a lot of fights in there because the testosterone is just high.

You can't negotiate with the people you are leading. It's gonna be hell. They're gonna be pushed beyond anything they've ever imagined. In order for me to get there, I have to use toughness and fear during that period. For instance, lining up for sprints. I tell them, usually at a high decibel level, "Never mind your feet. If your hands are not behind the start line, the whole team's got extra work." That's a moment when fights would break out. The players all have their horror stories. "Man, we ran thirty-one 110s in the stadium in hundred-degree weather." That's the summer, when it was just me in charge and no other coaches were around.

That did happen. But that team also won back-to-back national championships.

"The first day of practice, you hear Cochran's coaches saying, 'Don't worry about being tired.

Worry about getting better,'" Dont'a Hightower said. He won two national championships at Alabama and three Super Bowls with the New England Patriots. "You go out there and you remember them saying that while you're running your sprints. The next day, you realize you're not as tired as you were yesterday. What's the difference? I listened."

When the freshmen arrived, their first thought of me was that I was crazy. I was loud. They heard this strength coach making the team do extra because someone touched his knees. You know, "I'm throwing up, and he's still making me run." They can't believe we ran that much. But as Ginger Gilmore reminded me, the freshmen would see the relationship I had with the seniors and fall right into line. She called it my bedside manner. The players found out, as they got to know me, that I'm coming from a place of love. The tough times are just part of it.

"Because they trust him," Steve Sarkisian said about me, "they'll work their ass off for him. And once he gets their trust, he knows when to get in their face and ride them hard. He knows when to laugh with them. He knows when to back off. That's the skill set in and of itself."

SKULL SESSION

Michael Williams came to Alabama in one of the greatest class of recruits ever at any school, the 2008 class that included Hightower, Julio Jones, Mark Ingram, Marcell Dareus, Mark Barron, Barrett Jones, Courtney Upshaw, Terrence Cody, and I'm sure I'm leaving someone out. The ones who stayed five years may have won three national championships at Alabama, but I can tell you they didn't start out as future NFL stars. Michael reminded me how much he struggled with the conditioning drills his first week on campus. Struggled, as in I pulled him by his shorts to get him across the finish line of the drills. When he had enough air to talk, I told him to say, "I'm going to be great." I made him repeat it for two minutes. We didn't discuss it again until the clock hit 0:00 at the end of the 42–14 victory over Notre Dame in the Orange Bowl that won the 2012 BCS title, the third one in four seasons. I waded into the middle of the celebration, found Michael, and said, "What did I tell you?"

It would have been easy to berate a freshman who isn't in college football shape. That's low-hanging fruit. I chose to make a connection. I wanted our players to know that I cared about them. I committed to spending time with them when it was convenient for them, not just when I didn't have anything else going on. That meant a lot of nights—these guys love stuff at night. They'd come in to work out, and I'd be able to pick them off, grab them for a sit-down in my office. Or if we were in the middle of a workout and I saw them struggling, I'd pull them into the office after the workout. Kids are obvious. It's not like they play poker. When they struggle, it's written all over their faces. You don't go with tough love. You go with love. You go with motivation.

You crank up the music. You make it exciting. You give them something to be motivated about.

Once you make that connection, you can say tough things without losing their trust. Marlon Humphrey has played eight seasons at cornerback for the Baltimore Ravens. He's a two-time All-Pro. He came to Alabama in 2014 as a five-star recruit, all 179 pounds of him. He remembers me looking at him on his recruiting visit and saying, "We gotta get the butt right, man!" As in, he didn't have one. Football players (and everyone else, for that matter) generate power from the glutes, the hamstrings, the hips. Not having that foundation is not unusual for teenaged defensive backs. Marlon redshirted his first season and slipped into the funk that I described earlier: overachiever doesn't play, loses motivation, and so on. I'm pretty sure he didn't realize he had settled. I walked by him one day in the weight room, tapped him on the shoulder, and asked him, "Why you being a bitch?"

"The biggest thing that Cochran did was make people realize what they didn't realize," Marlon said.

"You might not know you're being negative. You might not know you're not as motivated as you once were. You might not know you're acting this way. That's the thing. Cochran was never going to lie to you. He was going to tell you the truth.

"I don't know if I even said anything back. I don't know if I just walked away. I just went back to my dorm. Once I thought about it, I realized I was just kind of in a fog, something that only somebody who cared about you could tell. Not that you're not working hard, but you might not be as motivated as you once were. The fire underneath you is still lit a little bit, but it's not as fiery as it should be. That's when I changed my mindset. I actually changed my phone screen and background to 'Nobody cares. Work harder.' That was really a big turning point for me in my career. You gotta keep working. Nobody really cares that you redshirted, nobody cares about whatever excuse you're trying to make. All you can do is work really hard and let the chips fly where they fly. I went on that next year to start, and the next year I went in the first round of the [NFL] draft.

"That was the thing about Cochran. He didn't have to tell me that. If you wanted to have success, if you wanted to win, if you wanted to be a great player, and you let it be known that's what you wanted to do, he wasn't really going to let you slip. I really appreciated him for that."

You think that doesn't mean the world to me?

"He listened to us," Dont'a Hightower said about me. "He was like a brother and an uncle. A granddad. He was all of those roles. He wanted to make sure that no matter what, he knew that he was doing what was in our best interest. Even if it was something he knew Nick wouldn't like. He was going to stand ten toes down, be in your corner."

SKULL SESSION

Choosing love over fear is a greater commitment. You're opening your heart to 105 players, every single one.

Somebody has to pay. For me, it was my family. I would get home, and the phone would ring. It'd be a parent I had been talking to all week, or a player dealing with one issue or another. As I said, these big, strong players may become national celebrities, but they aren't quite grown up yet. Our locker room had the complete range of emotional issues that young people have. We've had cutters. That's an eye opener, because you see the scars, and they're scary-looking. I always suspected the guys who wore sleeves in the weight room did so to hide their work.

The science shows that the frontal lobe of the cerebral cortex is not fully developed in males until twenty-five years of age. Their peers really affect how they think. They struggle to make decisions on their own. They need guidance. I decided that we should teach them. *Your peers affect how you make decisions. Let's talk about it. When everybody around you is smoking weed, you gotta stand on your own two feet or, as Dont'a said, ten toes down. When you go back home, what are you gonna do?*

Some kids solved that by not going home. My house became a haven for our players. I had a big house on the Indian Hills golf course in Tuscaloosa. I'd have them stay at the house sometimes. Every player I brought to the house found comfort being in a home setting. My kids were little at the time; being around Beau, Savannah, and Lucy got our players out of their own heads. Little kids will do that.

I had a big screen TV downstairs and set up chairs for the guys to play video games. They would come over, and I wouldn't even know they were there. They would park in the back and come in through the back door. I don't think we ever locked it.

Beau would come upstairs on a Saturday in the summer.

"What you been doing, Beau?"

"I was just playing Xbox with Damien Harris."

"Oh, he's down there?"

"Yeah, him and Jaylen Waddle."

"Okay. When did they get here?"

"I think they slept here, Dad."

"Cool."

I can tell you the Cochrans had plenty at the house for the three-day Christmas break. Bo

SKULL SESSION

Scarbrough, who's on my staff at West Alabama, and Tony Brown spent Christmas with me every year. They came to Christmas Eve Mass at 10 p.m., and then we went to Waffle House. That was our tradition. They were always with us.

I wanted our guys to trust me. I wanted them to trust each other. I wanted to maintain an atmosphere of trust that would invite the younger guys to buy in to what we did. It became easy for them to buy in when they saw former players like Julio Jones and Derrick Henry training with us every summer. Some pro alums would jump into the team workouts. Other would just work in their position group. The wide receiver group might have Julio and Terrell Owens. They are really close, so T.O. was always around. Those two were freaks, even when T.O. was forty years old.

The benefits were obvious. They served as great role models. You couldn't find a better recruiting aid. Come to Alabama—this is who you work out with. They didn't intimidate the young players. They spent a lot of time with them. I would have barbecues at the house, and the NFL guys came to expect them: "When are you cooking for the team?" That's what I would do on Saturdays. I'd make pancakes from 9 to 11, hamburgers from 11 to 1. Those are my two specialties. I can cook pancakes and hamburgers all day.

Julio is such a grinder, and he would train only with me. He wouldn't train with any of my assistants. I loved it, because he's such a joy to be around. Julio is just like Coach Saban. His personality is chill unless you're talking about football or business, just like Coach. They're very similar in that way.

When DeVonta Smith, Jaylen Waddle, and Jerry Jeudy were young wideouts and got to know Julio, they loved him. They saw that Julio went to the field for four hours a day. He would train with me for two hours, then he would go to the field and do drills, all football related, for four hours. The defensive backs, guys like Patrick Surtain or Minkah Fitzpatrick, would be out there doing DB drills, and Julio would say, "Come over here. We can work on stuff together." For instance, he'd be working on the top of his route that day. He would focus on just those two or three steps and explain to the DBs how he used those steps to gain separation.

Those young wideouts would see that, and they would beg me, "Can I miss class to train with them?" Once in a while, I'd get lazy enough to say yes.

All in all, having the players' trust allowed me to break down the walls that our players put up. Take 2018, when Alabama had two great quarterbacks and only one starting job. The previous season, veteran Jalen Hurts had led us to the College Football Playoff national championship. But at halftime Georgia led 13–0, so Coach Saban decided to make a change. He put freshman Tua Tagovailoa into the game, and Tua not only led our comeback, but he threw a 41-yard touchdown pass on our second play in overtime to beat Georgia and win our fifth national championship.

It remains one of the great moments not only in Alabama football history but in the history of the entire sport. It also drilled a few potholes in the road ahead of us. We entered 2018 with what appeared to be two great quarterbacks. In reality, Jalen had to figure out how to cope with losing his job, while Tua had to deal with being a statewide hero and a national star even though he had barely played. All the college football fan saw was the guy who completed second and 26 to win the national championship. Tua completely freaked out. He didn't know what to do, couldn't function, feared he would bobble the first snap—that's what whirled through his head.

Jalen wanted to redshirt, save the year of eligibility rather than play backup. I encouraged him not to do that. I kept telling him, "Be prepared. I don't know when, I don't know how, but you're gonna go in and win a game for us." I started calling him Superman, the hero who saves the world when everything is dire.

We always kept an eye on Georgia, whom we would play only if both teams won their divisions and reached the SEC Championship Game. Jalen bought in, and all season long, we told each other it would be against Georgia. The whole first half, as Georgia jumped two touchdowns ahead of us, a lot like they had done in the national championship game the season before, Jalen kept grabbing someone's glasses, putting them on, and coming over to me to say "Superman's ready. Superman's ready."

Sure enough, Tua got hurt. Jalen entered the game, and in the fourth quarter, he threw for one touchdown and ran for another, and we won, 35–28.

One other story from early in that game: Tight end Irv Smith Jr. dropped a third-down pass. The

SKULL SESSION

ball was perfectly thrown, and he jumped instead of just catching it. Irv dropped it right by our sideline. He came to the sideline with his head down, so distraught he lost track of the game. Irv played on the punt team. It was fourth down. We were punting. I grabbed him and said, "Dude, punt! We're still playing!"

After the punt, he came to the bench, sat down, and refused to look at me. I followed him, and said, "I'm not quitting. Look me in the eyes."

He picked up his glance and looked at me.

"You're gonna catch the next ball," I said. "I don't know if it's a five-yard out. I don't know if it's a swing pass. I don't know what it is, but you're gonna get another ball thrown to you, and you have to catch it. You're not the first guy that's ever dropped a ball at the University of Alabama, I promise. Even the NFL guys drop balls. You're gonna have to catch the next one, so get your head out of your ass. The next play is coming."

You have to be mentally tough not to dwell on the if-only, not to make excuses. Naturally you're going to think about them. You're human. We don't coach robots. But if you do everything you can, you won't think about the what-ifs as much.

LOVE, NOT FEAR

Irv did catch the next pass, a 3-yard gain on the next possession. More important, in the fourth quarter, he caught passes that converted a third and long on each of the two touchdown drives that Jalen led. I couldn't have been prouder of him.

Jalen and Tua are two very different cats with two very different problems, but my approaches to each of them remained similar. "You're great at football," I told them. "I can't wait to watch you play. I love when you have the ball in your hands." That positive reinforcement took the pressure off both of them. It took them back to the days when they played for the fun of it. I'm pretty sure positive reinforcement got Irv Smith's head back into the game, too.

No matter the industry, no matter the stakes, all of us respond to people who believe in us. We gain confidence from them. We don't want to let them down. It takes a little more emotional energy. But I've got eight rings that prove the approach works.

TEN

POSITIVE SELF-TALK

Positive self-talk is a game-changer. I guess I could say that about all of the methods I use in a Skull Session because they're all important. But I am by nature an optimist, a trait that has served me well, so I love positive self-talk.

I hated conditioning when I was playing. Hated it. It was the worst. All I wanted to do was lift and get big. Once I figured out what I needed to say to myself to go do the conditioning work, it became easy. What did I figure out? I said to myself that I didn't want to wear a suit to work every day. I saw my dad leave the house super early in the morning wearing a suit, I saw him come home that evening in a suit, and I did not want to live my life in a suit. Once I said that to myself, I could run all day. I don't think he ever resented being an example of what I didn't want to do. I hope not, anyway.

You have to find your words for yourself that get you in the zone, so that no matter what's going on, no matter how tough things get, you can lock in. There's science behind it. A lot of sports psychologists will tell you that berating yourself over and over again detracts from your goal. You ever listen to professional golfers? There's no sport that attacks you psychologically more than golf. The top guys on the PGA Tour are really good about eliminating negative thoughts.

They don't say they missed a putt. They say, "I hit a good putt. It didn't go in."

It takes practice. It takes going through the hard stuff, learning how to transform that experience into words that will reinforce you. If you control your vocabulary, you start feeling better. You start being able to perform better.

In my early days of recovery, when I couldn't sleep and felt like I had the flu and didn't know if I'd ever feel good again, I had to pull myself together well enough to get on a Zoom staff meeting with

POSITIVE SELF-TALK

my fellow coaches and act as if it were just another day. I had to find the words I needed to use to get through that Zoom. I just kept telling myself,

"I feel great."

"I feel great."

"I feel great."

"I feel great."

Over and over again I said it until I started to feel great, at least until the Zoom ended.

I say "I feel great" when my back goes out and I can't get out of bed. I lie in bed and say it until the snooze alarm goes off. Then I pop straight up and it doesn't hurt anymore. I say it when I cut onions. This guy, the guy who doesn't cry, can't slice onions without tears streaming down my face. Onions have my number. I started saying "I feel great" the moment I grab the knife. I cut two full onions without a tear. By the third onion, I started thinking there must be something wrong with these onions. If you can learn what to say to yourself when things get tough, if you can find your words, you'll be unstoppable.

One of the earliest demonstrations of positive self-talk I saw in my career came when I worked for the Hornets. Byron Scott, our head coach, had been an excellent shooting guard in the NBA for fifteen seasons, mostly with the Los Angeles Lakers. He won three rings on those great Showtime teams. I remember him telling a story about a shooting slump that bothered him enough that he decided to speak to someone—a therapist, not a shooting coach.

The therapist asked him, "What do you say when you hit a shot?"

"Bam!" Byron said. "Because it hits the back of the net." He didn't need to find more than that one word. Even when he participated in a shootaround with the players he coached, you'd hear him saying "Bam! Bam! Bam!" on every shot.

Finding your word or words locks you in. It eliminates stress, too. Julio Jones, one of the best wide receivers of the modern era, would say, "See the X, tuck." The X is the end of the football, where the seams come together. See the X, tuck the ball where the defense can't get at it. When Julio got overwhelmed in a game, when he questioned himself, like, say, after a drop, he would say, "See the X, tuck." When Jerry Jeudy got into a slump in the NFL, he borrowed Julio's saying. Once he saw the X and tucked, he stopped dropping passes.

POSITIVE SELF-TALK

Several years into my career at Alabama, the NCAA decided that every strength and conditioning coach had to be certified by an organization. Out of the blue, I had to take a test. I felt about tests the way I felt about having a job that called for wearing a suit. I'm not a good test taker, but I had to sit down and take a test. I didn't have a lot of positive self-talk going through my head. I spent a lot of time thinking I had no shot at passing the test. Every time I sat down to study, all I thought was *I could be playing with my kids, or I could be training my guys, and instead I'm sitting here on a Sunday, spending three hours out of my tiny stash of free time on this test.*

I had to find my words. I just said to myself, *Back to the test.* That refocused me. I might get only a good fifteen minutes of study before my mind began to wander again, but that was fifteen minutes I had no shot of getting otherwise.

The best way I can explain why this works is that positive self-talk means you are speaking to your brain instead of listening to it. Trust me, your brain can talk. It's going a million miles an hour, especially in stressful moments. Not only is it bouncing all over the map, but it's landing in some negative places. Why listen to that? You have a choice. It's much more enjoyable, not to mention much healthier, to listen to positive thinking. It's a skill that you have to develop. Our attention spans are shorter these days. That's what smartphones have done to us, especially to the age group that I coach. It's a grind to get them to focus. I tell our players that they've got to find their words, and they have to talk to themselves. If all you're going to do is listen, you're liable to hear, *Oh, my hamstring hurts! Oh, my back hurts! There's no way I can do this workout. I'm a Division II player; there's no way I can make it to the NFL.* That's not only negative talk, but it is also projecting far into the unknown. Remember, you have to think about *this* play or *that* drill. Be where your feet are.

What's the trick to finding the words? Your mantra has got to be short. It's got to be a shortcut to your "why." Once you know your why, then you can attach your words to it. Kevin Elko told the team at Alabama about Jaromír Jágr, the great Czech hockey player. Jagr wore number 68 for the Pittsburgh Penguins to commemorate the 1968 uprising by citizens against the Communist government. That was his why.

POSITIVE SELF-TALK

I've had a lot of players say that their why is "I gotta feed my family," or "Get my mom out of work." That's their why, so that's their talk. That's what they're saying to themselves. *Things are going to get difficult; they always do. I've got a midterm the next day. It's so hard, I'm going to stay up late studying. If I remind myself of the why, that I gotta feed my family, then, poof, I don't mind cranking the long hours.* The pain is gone. Greg McElroy, Coach Saban's first national championship–winning quarterback, said, "Why do you play football? To try to win is great. But you have to find a motivation deeper than that on February 12 in the middle of the Fourth Quarter conditioning program. Winning is not enough to get you where you need to be."

We had our players share their whys with one another. It not only deepened their bond, but it also gave them the chance to help one another. If I'm out there running that fifteenth sprint with you, and you're flagging, I can get you out of it. I can remind you of your why.

Another benefit is the power of routine. You attach your words to your why, and you repeat them. It's just like the best golfers do with their preshot routines, except that theirs are physical. They perform the same movements, and they stick with their routine. That's what we do with positive self-talk. You stick with one thing. It becomes your mantra. The Los Angeles Chargers punter JK Scott started for us for four years at Alabama. In the first half of his sophomore year, 2015, he got into a rut. For a punter, the ball drop is critical. He's got to drop it directly to the inside of the foot, without the ball dipping, without spin.

I asked JK, "When you nail the drop, what do you say to yourself?"

"There it is," he said.

He knew what a good drop looked like. And he knew that he got the drop right, he said, "There it is." Why not feel the good vibes that came with saying that? JK already had chosen his words and didn't even realize it. He didn't just think *There it is*. He said it out loud every time he dropped the ball. That's how you become a veteran punter in the NFL.

The beauty of positive self-talk is that, like just about everything we discuss in a Skull Session, its benefits are not limited to football. Look at it this way: Positive self-talk basically is a mantra. We all

POSITIVE SELF-TALK

have deadlines to meet, sales to make. We all have numbers to hit. Whatever it is you've got to do, you've got to find something that will lock you in to make that right call.

Notice that all of these mantras share a common trait. There are no negative thoughts. Julio doesn't say "Don't drop this ball." JK doesn't say "Don't drop this ball wrong." You can't say a negative. Your mind will hear the negative, sniff it out like a bird dog. There's a rap song I considered using in my weight room with the lyric "I don't get tired." I didn't use it. All your mind's going to hear is *tired*. We had three words that we never allowed anyone to say during any workout, practice, meeting, or within my earshot: *hot*, *tired*, and *can't*. No one needs to hear those. I can look at you and see that you're not in shape yet. I know you're coming in at three hundred or four hundred pounds. I know you can't do ten pull-ups. But we're gonna find a way. So don't say *can't*. I can tell that you've been up late studying all night. I know we're in two-a-days. I know you're tired. There's no reason to tell anybody. It's 110 degrees outside. No shit. It's hot. I don't need to hear it. Find a different language, because your language holds a lot of strength in your mind, right? If you're saying "I'm tired, I'm hot," you make it very difficult to achieve your goal. You say "I'm tired, I'm hot, I'm tired, I'm hot," enough, you're gonna lay out.

Coach Saban always used the frying pan story with our players. He would describe a fishing trip back home in West Virginia, where he grew up. Coach saw this guy fishing next to him, and the guy kept catching these huge trout. He'd reel them in, take a look at them, shake his head, and release them back into the river. Coach couldn't help himself. He went over to the guy and asked, "Why are you throwing the big fish back into the lake?"

And the guy said, "Because my frying pan's only this big."

Coach would always ask the players, "How big is your frying pan?" I love that story because it made the players laugh and think. It got the point across. You and the people you lead have to be ready for success. Positive self-talk prepares all of us for that moment when the door opens to our biggest dreams. We're ready to walk right through it.

ELEVEN

CATFISHING YOUR WAY TO LEADERSHIP

It doesn't matter whether you're a football team, a sales team, or an educational team. If you're a group of people trying to achieve a common goal, you need to develop leadership. Leadership is a skill like any other. Exercises that develop leadership are effective because they teach your people to hone their communication skills. If your players, teammates, or colleagues trust you and believe that you believe in them, they will follow you when you point the way toward the future.

One of the best leadership exercises I learned from Kevin Elko is called catfish. It's not a reference to the internet scam of someone assuming a fake identity in order to trick someone into thinking they're in a romantic relationship. (Not for nothing, but that is some sick stuff.)

This catfishing refers to the old-time practice of putting a catfish in a shipment full of cod. The catfish keeps the cod moving. The idea behind the exercise is to keep your people moving, prevent them from being satisfied. The way it works is that in a meeting setting, in front of everyone, your peers tell you two good things you're doing and one thing you need to improve.

At Alabama, a coach would start the session by telling a player to stand up and saying something like "You know, when you're on, you bring the whole team with you. You're really good at third down. You would be an All-American if you went to class every day."

That player comes to the front of the room and he picks a teammate and does the same thing—gives him two things he's doing well and calls him out on a third. And on you go through the group of players. We usually did it in position groups, to take advantage of the relationships they already have. In addition, it's not so many players that the room loses focus.

It sounds like a daytime TV talk show, but the vibe is completely different. The players in the "studio audience" are not hooting and hollering. Far from it. The room is quiet. *Everybody* is quiet because they're afraid they're going to get called on. They're terrified.

There are some methods we used to make the process work at its best. First, the coach who starts the process calls on a leader, a player respected by everyone in the room. One of the leaders you must develop is your point person. In our case, that means the quarterback. He has to be the team leader. The team benefits from his leadership. It's neither a surprise nor coincidence that Coach Saban's quarterbacks became excellent leaders.

Defensive teams had leaders, too. Often it would be a middle or inside linebacker, the guy responsible for calling signals and getting the defense in the right scheme. Offensive and defensive leaders worked together, held each other accountable.

On our first national championship team, in 2009, quarterback Greg McElroy became a great leader. He showed serious grit. He played in the BCS national championship game with hairline fractures in a couple of ribs. If you say, "Only hairline fractures?" you've never had one.

There were times when McElroy would come to the sideline after throwing a bad ball, mad at himself, or after taking a tough hit, and his head would be somewhere else. Dont'a Hightower or Rolando McLain, the defensive leaders, would jump on him, tell him to get it together. Greg would snap out of his funk. "I'm okay, I'm fine," he'd say, almost like he needed to shake out the cobwebs or something. He would get with whatever offensive coach he needed to get with. On we went.

In a catfish exercise, you start with your leader because he can take the criticism. The leader then takes a guy who trusts him, who knows that whatever he says is coming from a good place, and you keep doing that through the leaders in the group. Suddenly all your leaders are standing in front of the room. They have established their credibility and the credibility of the process. They have had their egos stroked and taken constructive criticism, and everyone in the room knows how it works. That's when you start in on the guys who need to hear the criticism.

"Man, you've got insane athletic ability, you could really help us in this or that situations, but you can't get right on what you're doing off the field." That guy comes up to the front, and selects one of his teammates, and catfishing gets really interesting.

Another way to do it is that the coach does all the leaders in the room, and once they're up there, he asks, "Who do y'all want to catfish?" Each one of them will pick someone and give him the positive-positive-negative. Together, they feel confident that they can talk to a guy. They're going to go straight to the guy that can help the team but is just not mature enough to get out of his own way yet.

The catfish exercise utilizes strength in numbers without straying into bullying. No player is hearing from more than one other player. Having said that, the process can throw a string of firecrackers into the room. It's always powerful. We usually did it in preseason camp, when we tried to cement the ethic of the team. When a young guy on our team hears something like "Man, when you're pumped up, you motivate me," and that young guy is a sophomore who hasn't touched the field, he's going to listen to the rest of the message: "But this is the reason why I haven't seen you on the field yet." It turns what could sound like criticism into a motivational message. The older players are giving the younger guy confidence, and they're giving him permission to be great.

I'll give you an example. I remember Mark Barron telling Dre Kirkpatrick, "My man, you're fast and you can play. You could really help us. You could start as a freshman. You're too worried about what everybody else thinks about you." That one sticks in my head.

Mark is wired differently than most. He came to Alabama mentally tough. He was only a year ahead of Dre. In fact, he was actually a day younger than Dre. But when Dre showed up for summer seven-on-seven workouts, Mark kicked him off the field a couple of times. Dre would trash-talk the wideouts, and Mark would say, "We don't do that here, man. Get off the field." Mark Barron is very much a speak-softly-and-carry-a-big-stick guy. But when you mess with him on the football field? Whew, get out of his way! He's a monster.

Camp started, and we get to the catfish session, and everybody knows that Mark is going to call on

Dre. And they're all waiting, because they know that Mark is going to drill Dre, hit him right in the numbers. He's been on Dre's ass the whole summer. Instead, Mark told him, "You know you could help us, and I'm hard on you *because* you can help us. You're a good enough player, but you too worried about all this other stuff."

Dre Kirkpatrick got a lot of playing time as a freshman, so people listened to him. But he complained a lot. He didn't always do what was right. He was "cool." Eventually the messaging seeped into his skull. He became a starter at corner the next season in the defensive backfield, alongside Mark at safety. Dre came out of Alabama after his junior year, when he made All-American alongside Mark. Dre went seventeenth in the 2012 NFL Draft, ten picks after Mark.

It's important to point out that catfishing is not an exercise to attempt before you've established the ground rules of your culture. If your people haven't bought in to your vision, to what you believe they have to do to get to where you want to go, you may end up with bad feelings. You have to know who you are, and your people should be open to hear what their colleagues tell them, because as a team,

SKULL SESSION

you've been working on your gratitude. You know one another's why. You know the DNA traits of the organization.

Another way I tried to develop leaders was spending more time with them. I tried to be close to every player, but I felt like I had to cultivate the leaders we had. I started having leadership lunches in my office. That became a thing around 2012, with Barrett Jones and AJ McCarron. Barrett was a coach's dream, a driven offensive lineman who had the skills and the intellect to play every position on the offensive line. He made All-American as a tackle. He made All-American as a center and won the Campbell Trophy, often considered to be the academic Heisman. AJ, our quarterback, also was a natural-born leader who started for us for three seasons.

AJ and Barrett always came to eat their lunch in my office between workout groups during the season, and they just would go at each other the way that brothers do.

Late in our 42–14 victory over Notre Dame for the 2012 BCS championship, AJ lined up behind Barrett, who played center that year, and they got into an argument over the protection call, both of them so headstrong that we had to call timeout and pretty much had to separate them. Keep in mind, we had a four-touchdown lead in the fourth quarter of the national championship game, the final game of the season.

That's leadership.

The beauty of coaching college athletes is that you help boys mature into men. The problem is that as soon as you get leaders developed, they walk out the door, and you've got to have guys in place behind them. To kick-start that process, we used to take twenty or so players every spring to a leadership retreat at Sweet Apple Farms, a hunting and fishing camp about forty-five minutes west of Tuscaloosa that the Fellowship of Christian Athletes uses. It's a few miles north of the University of West Alabama, where I'm coaching now.

We made it a privilege to be selected to go. You had to have playing time, so we usually had juniors and seniors, although we always brought three or four quarterbacks regardless of their age and playing experience. Remember, quarterbacks *have* to lead.

The point of the conference is to figure out who your leaders are. From the twenty players who went

SKULL SESSION

to Sweet Apple Farms, Coach Saban would select a dozen players to be the official leadership group of the team that fall. The attendees he didn't select for leadership remained on the group text thread. That way you're cultivating the next class of leaders. We wanted the players to want to be in the leadership group. We wanted it to be cool.

We did a lot of bonding exercises, like playing paintball in teams, only no one could speak. You had to learn how to communicate without speaking. That was always really good, because once they have permission to speak, they realize you have to be a vocal leader to communicate. I used to tell the players, "Y'all are afraid to speak up, but you got freshmen teammates who don't even know what color socks they're supposed to wear. Communicate! Speak! That's what leaders do." It can seem cool not to be the leader, to not show that you care. That's *not* what leaders do.

If one player has the cojones to get everybody around him to shut up and say, "Hey, listen up," then he's a leader. If another player is speaking to the team, get behind him. Have his back. Get everybody around to listen. It's easy to be the one making the smartass remark. If a player has the leader's back, and gets people around him to be quiet, then they see he's a leader when all he's doing is listening. I would tell our older guys, "Whether you like it or not, the young guys look at you as a leader, because you've played, and they're trying to do things like you, just like you watched the guys ahead of you."

All of these concepts are not only relevant to football. They are universal truths about leadership. For instance, we made sure to bring our naturally gifted public speakers into the leadership process. If you don't do that, they can destroy your team. They may not mean to destroy anything. But they're the first ones to complain, the first ones to do something stupid. We would bring those guys to the leadership conference, not because we thought they could be leaders but because they had juice. We wanted them rowing in the same direction as everyone else. That was Coach Saban's big thing. The player's not a leader, but he's got a lot to say, people listen to him because he's played a lot, and he's outgoing. He may have some issues, but he can get the attention of the meeting room or the locker room, so let's get him in there and teach him this stuff. He can see how his words give him power.

He can learn how to use his words in in a positive way.

We made sure we brought Dre into our leadership process, which helped him a lot. Dre saw himself as a follower. We brought him to Sweet Apple Farms. The process helped him see himself as a leader. We gave him permission to lead. We gave him permission to keep the standard high.

When we played Arkansas and Dre had an interception to win the game, he came into the locker room as a different person. He was less showy. He had gotten beat, but he came back to make the pick to close the game out. His attitude was "That was close. I need to buckle up." He grew up. That was pretty cool.

Most of the guys you tried to bring into the tent stayed in the tent. There's a zebra-changing-his-stripes quality to the process. But if they strayed, you just reel them back in. "Bro, we talked about this. We talked about this multiple times. You can't do that. Come on, man."

Jeff Allen once said that he considered me to be built for college athletics, that what gives me joy is helping people. He said that's why the NFL didn't hold much interest for me, because those players are grown men, and these kids that he and I work with are craving the help we can give them, even if they don't always know it. That's pretty much what Coach Saban found out when he went to the NFL, too. There aren't many things in life more satisfying than molding young people.

TWELVE

HEAD COACH

When West Alabama hired me, AJ McCarron called me and said, "Fifteen years ago, you said you were gonna be a head coach. You said it in your office. Look at you now. You finally got it."

I don't remember saying that to him, but I'm not surprised that I said it. The fact that I was a strength coach and that being a strength coach is not the shortcut to becoming a head coach didn't stop me.

I hope I have made it clear that I now understand that my original pursuit of a head coaching gig was fueled by my desire for money and power. My ego drove that bus. Only when I put aside my ego and reordered my life did I become a head coach. Is that crazy? Maybe not. It's like God said, "Now you're ready." Or else He's saying, "Okay, Mr. Humble. Be careful what you wish for." Either way, I just don't take myself so seriously anymore. I no longer think that because I have been on eight national championship teams and gotten all this acclaim that I need to act a certain way. I felt that pressure at Georgia, all coming from a place of insecurity.

"I gotta prove I belong."

"I gotta prove that I can be a special teams coordinator."

I don't have to do that ever again. My faith has become my anchor. Every morning, I pray: "Please keep me sober" and "Thank you for waking me up." Now I try to say the rosary daily and spend a few quiet minutes with God. It's nothing crazy, but it makes all the difference.

We'll find out if I can succeed as a head coach. That's the cool thing about football. You find out every Saturday. It's very freeing. The next season will come, and we'll find out if I'm any good. And then the season after that will come, and we'll find out again. In football, you prove yourself every time you step on the field.

I urge you to look at your challenges, your goals, your dreams, the same way. How your last game or season or profit/loss sheet came out doesn't have to have a bearing on what's ahead of you. The road is never straight, and as I well know, it's not always paved very smoothly, either. There will be times when your brain tells you it's okay to quit. Sometimes, if you don't talk to your brain, someone else will do it for you. The late Mal Moore, whom I learned so much from during his time as athletic director at Alabama, used to tell the story of his freshman year playing for the new Crimson Tide coach, Paul "Bear" Bryant. Mal would come back from practice, walk to the pay phone in the hallway of his dorm, and call his dad.

"I quit. I can't play for this man, the Bear," Mal would say. "He's crazy. I can't play for him."

His dad told him, "You can't come back to Dozier, Alabama. You'll be fine."

A week later, Mal called home again. "I can't play for this man," he said. "I quit, I quit, I quit."

"Don't come back over here," his dad said. "I already turned your room into an office."

The only thing that Mal quit was calling home. He stuck it out. And here's the best part: If you

SKULL SESSION

don't quit, if you're going through something difficult, if you're pushing through things that are hard, you never know. Maybe one day, you'll have a building named after you. I worked in the Mal Moore Athletic Facility for thirteen years.

I can't promise you a building with your name carved into the façade, but that's not a goal, anyway. It's a much bigger version of a championship ring, something you get because of your success. There are as many different definitions of success as there are people trying to succeed. You picked up this book looking for help in achieving your definition of success. I can promise you that the strategies that I have laid out for you are effective. I believe in them. I believe in you. If your organization has the right DNA traits and sets SMART goals, if you show your people that you love them and have their back, if you can explain to them the benefit of speaking positively to themselves, you'll get where you want to go. You'll be prepared to take advantage of the good fortune that will come your way. Nobody can be luckier than a twenty-seven-year-old strength coach who gets the opportunity to work for the best college football coach of our lifetime. But it was the tools I had and the skills I learned that allowed me to *keep* working for him. It's pretty obvious that I've had bad things happen to me, too. But I'm good. I'm playing the next play. I'm right where my feet are.

ACKNOWLEDGMENTS

I would like to thank my friends and former players who added their memories of my career to my own: Jeff Allen, Preston Dial, Ginger Gilmore, Dont'a Hightower, Marlon Humphrey, Josh Maxson, Greg McElroy, Jeff Purinton, Freddie Roach, Steve Sarkisian, and Damion Square. And, of course, my wife, Cissy, for her help in telling my story. I can't thank her enough.

ABOUT THE AUTHORS

SCOTT COCHRAN is a force of nature. He redefined what it means to be a strength and conditioning coach and helped build two college football dynasties. For over two decades, he was the pulse behind the powerhouse programs of LSU, Alabama, and Georgia, collecting eight national championships and shaping the careers of many legends. Cochran is now the head football coach at West Alabama. He is also the leading voice behind Eliminate the Whisper, a movement by the American Addiction Recovery Association, which he co-founded, to combat the stigma of mental health and addiction struggles, and he's sharing his message far and wide.

IVAN MAISEL has covered college football for more than four decades, most prominently at ESPN from 2002 to 2021. He served as editor-at-large for *ESPN College Football 150*, the multiplatform

ABOUT THE AUTHORS

history project that in 2019 commemorated the sport's sesquicentennial. Maisel also covered college football for *Sports Illustrated*, *Newsday*, and *The Dallas Morning News*. He has written four books, including *I Keep Trying to Catch His Eye*, a memoir of dealing with grief after the death of his son in 2015. His latest book, *American Coach: The Triumph and Tragedy of Notre Dame Legend Frank Leahy*, will be published by Grand Central in September 2025.